All is Relative

Aart Jurriaanse

All is Relative

A Revelation of Man's Cosmic Connections

BRIDGES
PUBLISHING

The Publisher wishes to acknowledge the support of Pat.

First Published in South Africa by Inner Space Publishing.

Cover Design by Rosi Weiss

Published 2026 by: in Cooperation with:
Bridges Publishing   "Sun Centre"
Hans-Juergen Maurer   School of Esoteric Philosophy
Frankfurt am Main   5, Almond Drive
Germany   Somerset West 7130
                               South Africa

www.maurer.press

ISBN 978-3-929345-21-6

Table of Contents

Part II   Life is Complex

About Copyright

These days very little literature is published without stressing the fact that the author is retaining the relative copyright. This may be justified when regarded purely from the commercial point of view, trying to ensure that no other party shall encroach and share in this potential source of profit.

When regarded, however, from a more altruistic and charitable aspect, it merely reflects the typical selfish attitude of the average human being, trying to ensure that every cent to which he might legally be entitled must be grasped and retained, with little or no concern as to the moral or rather humane approach.

A closer consideration of this insistence on the retention of copyright may, however, also disclose some other facts of the situation. There is for instance the case where it is felt that someone might abuse the right of freely availing himself of the writings of another, and that such a person should be prevented from committing literary piracy or plagiarism by availing himself of the exact words, or using direct quotations from such unprotected writings, without due acknowledgement of the source. It will be found, however, that in practice very little can be done to prevent others using the essence of such propounded thoughts, ideas or tenets, simply by effecting some elementary changes in words, sentences and their general context. Such procedure may sometimes result in badly distorting the meaning of the original writing, although in other instances a clearer and even improved version of the basic elements might actually be achieved.

The main argument for not retaining copyright on literary work, is based on the principle that the more worthy thoughts and ideas with which the mind of man is imbued, are not given to him for purely personal advantage and selfish retention, or to be converted into a suitable form for bartering to the highest bidder on the open market, nor to be commercialised in some other way. No, man should come to the realisation that the receiver of enlightened superior ideas is merely the instrument being used by Higher Authorities for enriching the life of mankind as a while. Instead of appropriating such knowledge solely for personal benefit or enrichment, the relative instrument should only feel honoured that he is being used as an effective channel, and that he is being granted the opportunity and privilege to serve his fellow men by bringing such information to wider public attention, and for satisfying some human need.

It should always be remembered that physical man is merely an instrument equipped with a sensitive mind and a material brain, which under certain circumstances may serve as an excellent computer. These human computers are being fed with a variety of data originating from many sources. In practice it is generally found that some of these instruments are better attuned to certain specific objectives, whereas others are again oriented towards other purposes, thus eventually covering the whole sphere of human need and endeavour. All these instruments, with their widely varying qualities and capacities, remain the channels used by Higher Authority for the distribution of the ever increasing flow of knowledge from Upper Regions for the evolutionary development not only of mankind, but of the complete range of manifested creation, of which the human kingdom only forms a part. It therefore behoves man to give his unstinted devotion and collaboration, enabling him to serve as an efficient tool for transmitting these energies, without allowing himself to become unduly obstructive by directing these gifts towards selfish needs or towards personal enrichment and glorification.

What has briefly been pointed out above with regard to the use of copyright, similarly applies to the closely related 'patent rights' which can be registered for obtaining the sole right to manufacture certain specific commodities. In these instances the so-called inventors or patent holders are abusing their privilege to serve as effective instruments or channels, by 'patenting' the concepts with which they have been entrusted, and which were intended to promote the interests of all humanity. Therefore, instead of freely sharing that with which they were endowed, these inventors often deprive their fellow men of their divine prerogatives by only disposing of these bequests when this can be effected at personal advantage.

It is realised that this petition for the more general and generous sharing of the inspirational thoughts and concepts with which man is being blessed, may sound unrealistic and even ridiculous to many, and that at this stage this appeal may only represent a few lone voices calling from the wilderness. Fortunately, however, there is a rapidly growing awareness that mankind is now entering a New Age which is demanding the introduction of fresh principles and a totally new approach to life. Under the circumstances it will therefore probably still take a while, but the time has now arrived for these ideas to be introduced, after which they will gradually gain support and eventually will prove acceptable.

Such a new outlook will, however, demand a much clearer understanding of the true nature of man, of his purpose in life, and of his eventual destiny. So much more must also become known about the energies by which he is motivated, their Source, and how they function. For present purposes let it suffice, however, that the future of mankind will necessarily have to be based on better human relationships, and therefore on deeper understanding, on goodwill and on sharing, ever keeping it in mind that one of the many practical and effective ways of achieving these objectives, will be to relinquish any undue claims for the registering or retaining of patents or copyright on items or elements which should be made available to mankind as freely as possible. The time is bound to come when posterity will look back with distaste or pity to the present 'dark age', and will be unable to understand how man could ever have had the presumption to appropriate and limit the 'Gifts of the Gods' for selfish and personal gain.

Please ponder on these thoughts and try to proclaim these principles whenever possible, thus making a further small contribution towards effecting the many changes required for the eventual realisation of all that is implied when referring to the New Age.

Under the circumstances there seems to be no alternative but to offer these thoughts for what they are worth, for free and unrestricted use to all-comers, and without subjecting them to any form of copyright!

PART I

Fundamentals of Existence

ALL IS ENERGY

All that Is, is Composed of Energy

This book is bound to contain thoughts and points of view which many will find contentious, because some of these assertions cannot be proved scientifically, being concerned with esoteric concepts stretching way beyond human perception and also beyond the recording capacity of the most sensitive of man-made instruments. Luckily, one of the most fundamental of these premises has during the course of recent years been lifted above the often sordid levels of controversy.

This most significant concept, which in the near future will assume every greater importance and stature as man progressively becomes aware of its deeper implications, is contained in that most significant adage that "All is Energy". The growing awareness amongst scientists of the truth of this ancient esoteric statement is now largely founded on scientific research and on conclusions that have emerged from activities associated with the 'atomic age' which mankind has entered, in which the fission of atoms of matter and the fusion of energies is playing such an important role.

The meaning of this simple dictum is obvious and relatively straightforward and what it amounts to is that every form of creation, of whatever nature, whether large or small, whether dense and material or of ephemeral and imperceptible consistency, in fact all that IS, is composed of energy. It is self-evident that such energy must vary considerably in quality or nature as well as in degree of concentration or state of compaction, to produce that infinite variety of form, quality and appearance in which both the tangible and intangible forms of creation are manifested.

The word 'energy' is today glibly bandied about by every man in the street, because the use of certain aspects of energy is increasingly playing such an economically important and therefore noticeable role in man's daily activities and especially in his several forms of transport. The energy normally referred to under these circumstances is the potential power contained in various 'fuels', which is released by the combustion or transmutation of such material in the many types of engines which man has devised for converting such fuels into motive or other manifestations of power.

With the course of time, especially during the past two centuries, man has taken great strides in availing himself of the many kinds of energy. He has become aware of many and varying types and qualities of energy and from year to year he is improving his techniques for applying these energies more effectively to fresh designs and new fields of human endeavour, which in many instances are creditable and to human benefit. But alas, all too frequently they are applied destructively or purely selfishly for promoting personal or sectional gain and that often to the detriment of the interests of mankind as a whole.

Notwithstanding the basic acceptance of the fact that all is energy, the average man still finds it difficult to realise that all forms of manifestation are energy forms, that each is composed of subsidiary forms and that in turn each form only constitutes a part of some more comprehensive body. Each of these forms, whether large or small, whether an atom or a solar system, is therefore an expression of varying conglomerations of energy and of energy subjected to innumerable states and degrees of bondage.

Energy in Perpetual Motion

Whatever the outer appearance of the energy form, it remains subject to another comprehensive natural law which man is inclined to disregard, namely that energy is a power which forever remains vibrantly alive, remaining in a perpetual state of movement, animation and fluctuation, even though to the human eye the manifested form may give the appearance of being perfectly stable and immutable. The consequence is that each and every form, no matter whether dense or evanescent, remains in a constant state of change, consistently exchanging energies with its surround by a reciprocal process of absorption and radiation. It is the rate at which this exchange of energy is taking place and the quality of the relative energies, which will eventually determine the tempo and degree of change effected.

A further result of this interchange of energies is that every form, whatever its nature, is to some extent being influenced by surrounding forms and similarly every structure, because of either its radiation or magnetism, will have some reciprocal influence on all that surrounds it.

The Interconnectedness of all Forms

And thus all forms of creation throughout the whole Universe are directly or indirectly linked by energy of some nature, forming a most wonderful and divine system of interdependence, where everything is consciously or unconsciously linked or associated by means of the etheric system and where all life is contingent on the circulation, transmission and interchange of the innumerable aspects and facets of manifested energy. These principles remain valid on all levels of existence, both spiritual and material and are applicable during the processes of involution, evolution and devolution. They are relevant to the Universe, the macrocosm, and are equally apposite to the microcosm of our solar system, or if reduced to still narrower limits, to the world of man on earth.

When referring to energy forms, the inclination is to visualise or think only of that which is material, but actually energy forms are reflected in a never ending variety of expression including both the dense and the ephemeral. There are for instance such things as thoughts, which notwithstanding their lack of tangible substance, can actually constitute most potent forms of energy concentration. Thoughts may in turn be expressed in a more substantial form such as speech, which although still intangible, can at least be registered by the human ear and can again be further transposed into the still more stable form of the written word or else into some other motivated form of activity or creation. All that is manifested is therefore supported in a sea of energy, which includes energy in the process of being involved into forms; energy that is impacting on existing forms, activating and evolving them according to some Divine Purpose towards an unknown but defined destiny; energy in the process of dissolution, thereby dissipating existing forms which have served their purpose and have to make way for that which is new. Energies released in the course of the latter process or which are being radiated by existing forms, will either be reabsorbed within the surround or else will disappear beyond the threshold of human perception, back into the illimitable unknown to continue its cyclic procession in fulfilment of Divine Purpose under direction of the Will of the SUPREME.

By contemplating these concepts, the dedicated student will arrive at some faint realisation of the majesty of the ordered activity and synthesis of our planetary existence in which the variety of energies are finding expression in the divine Life reflected in the several kingdoms of Nature.

Humanity's Role in the Transmission of Energy

Energy is indestructible and inexhaustible in extent and as it is being used or converted its supply will constantly be replenished. Energy proceeds on a cyclic course and although it may temporarily become bound or restricted into form, it must inevitably at some stage or other be released again into the greater reservoir, eventually to be redirected to fulfil some further function in a new field of expression. Man has been favoured with the power of consciously and deliberately availing himself of certain energies or in other instances of diverting or redirecting them. These powers may either be used beneficially and constructively or else abused – as energies are of a neutral nature, disposing of no subjective will or intelligence. They therefore remain obedient to guidance by will of qualified entities, whose direction may lead to either positive or negative results in accordance with the motivation.

The final goal of the esoteric student is consciously to become a focal point of energy which can be used by hierarchical workers as a convenient station for the reception, channelling and redirection of energies. The aspirant must therefore increasingly endeavour to cultivate and improve his sensitivity and therefore his powers of reception. For this purpose it is of first importance that his emotional aspects should be brought under firm control and that he should simultaneously develop a spiritual sense which will not only render him sensitive to impression, but will also allow him to become a pure and selfless channel for conveying and transmitting the energies received. He must therefore learn to live consciously in the world of energies, become aware of himself as a unit of energy integrated into a more comprehensive expression of energy – his community, which again forms part of humanity and eventually of the greater Whole. Without a clear recognition of the position he occupies in this greater system, he cannot function effectively and become a true instrument in the hands of the Masters. He must therefore come to the realisation that his world of energy in which he moves and has his being is merely a part of the manifested vehicle of our Planetary Logos and that the energies of which this complex is composed remain in a perpetual state of movement, which is focussed in various vortices of force, of which the Spiritual Hierarchy and Humanity are of prominent importance.

THE SOURCE AND NATURE OF ENERGY

Unrecognised Wonders of the Universe

Yes, familiarity breeds contempt. Man has become so accustomed to the presence of the sea of energy in which he is submerged and with the multiplicity of currents which are constantly activating him and with which he is continuously working, that much of this is taken for granted and accepted as the natural state of affairs. Only here and there an exceptional individual is found who has the required mental approach to ponder on the real nature of these energies, their meaning, source and purpose. But this apparent indifference is only natural, as the masses are not yet mentally inclined and cannot be bothered to think deeply about any subject, and most certainly not about matters which actually go beyond their understanding. But even the thinkers of the world, the philosophers and scientists, generally do not realise that they are in fact dealing with the greatest wonders and powers of the Universe. These remain unappreciated and unrecognised, man being unaware of the fact that he is granted the opportunity of collaborating with the expression and materialisation of the 'thoughts' and therefore the Divine Will and Energy of our Planetary Logos.

The Evasive Nature of Energy

But what is this 'Energy', this concept to which reference has so readily and repeatedly been made in the foregoing pages? To this question no human being can really give a satisfactory and conclusive answer – no, not even our greatest scientists. Energy may evasively be described as radiations or as a form of electricity or as life. But neither does man know what 'electricity' and 'life' are, of which only some qualities can be described or enumerated. The real essence of their being lies beyond human definition, because as an expression of Deity they surpass his understanding. It is a fact that electricity can be 'generated', but the word 'generate' in this instance is actually a misnomer and is deceptive because generating means creating and man does not freshly create electricity, but by means of his techniques he is merely gathering or concentrating existing electric energy from nature where it occurs in various states of diffusion. Similarly 'life' can be propagated in different ways, but it will be found that this merely remains a question of encouraging nature to multiply from existing focal points of life and never concerns the creating of life de novo. No, the honest scientist will acknowledge that the basic constituents or energies of nature, such as Life and electricity are really inexplicable and are merely accepted as part of that enigmatic and all-comprehensive Divine gift of Universal Energy of which every form of manifestation is an expression and in which every form is sustained, which simultaneously constitutes the medium for effecting these perpetual changes which man recognises as involution, evolution and finally devolution or the process of reabsorbing the energy concerned into the original matrix.

Origin of Energy from the Supreme Source

If the existence of this vital and universal expanse of Energy is accepted, then the next logical question arising in the exploring mind would be with regard to the source of these energies. But again these are metaphysical concepts transcending all human understanding and which can only tentatively be smoothed over by relatively inane and inadequate platitudes, such as stating that these energies are emanations from the Supreme Being, the Almighty, "The One About Whom Naught May be Said" and that they represent the medium for expressing His Supernal Will.

This brings us to a closer examination of the nature of this Divine Energy which is fundamental to all Creation. Fortunately for man, fresh sources of knowledge are progressively being revealed to him and some of this reaches far beyond the precincts and limitations of present day scientific thought. Today, there are a growing number of inspired scientists who no longer allow their minds to remain confined by the strictly 'proven' and therefore material concepts of the past and who are now tentatively beginning to explore metaphysical spheres of thought, which up till recent years remained a closed and forbidden terrain for every self-respecting scientist. The present study is principally based upon the teachings which have been presented to mankind by a Sage already well known to esoteric students as the Master Djwhal Khul or more intimately as 'The Tibetan', who telepathically dictated some ten thousand pages of script to his amanuensis, Alice A. Bailey. These dictations were taken down over a period of thirty years, between 1919 and 1949 and were progressively published in a series of eighteen textbooks, which have been listed in the Appendix.

The present version has been produced from studies of the Tibetan's original work and is merely an attempt at presenting the public with a simplified account of these teachings for the benefit of those who for some reason are unable to make a more profound study of the complete writings.

It should be clearly realised, however, that any attempt at interpreting or simplifying virginal teachings, immediately and inevitably reduces such teachings to a lower level. Therefore once the student has gained a reasonable insight into these thoughts, he should definitely turn his attention to the original writings for more profound discernment.

According to the Tibetan, the unprofaned energy emanating from the Supreme Being, is initially radiated into the Universe as a Trinity, consisting of the energies of the Father, the Son and the Holy Spirit, but these are subsequently split up and manifested as the Seven Rays of Divine Energy.

As each of these rays comes into contact with some celestial body, the Ray energy permeates that body, impregnating it with its qualities. In the process, the Ray energies are broken up again into seven subsidiary Rays of the same nature as the original Seven Rays, but now of a somewhat diminished potency, in which form the Rays proceed towards their next point of destiny. Within the course of tim and circumstances, this process is endlessly repeated, thus enabling the deepest and most hidden recesses of the Universe and to activate eventhe minutest forms of creation. At the same time, it must be kept in mind that every form at some earlier stage of evolution has been the product or creation of previous Rays of Energy, specifically directed towards such purpose by a particular Instance or Entity.

THE SUPREME BEING

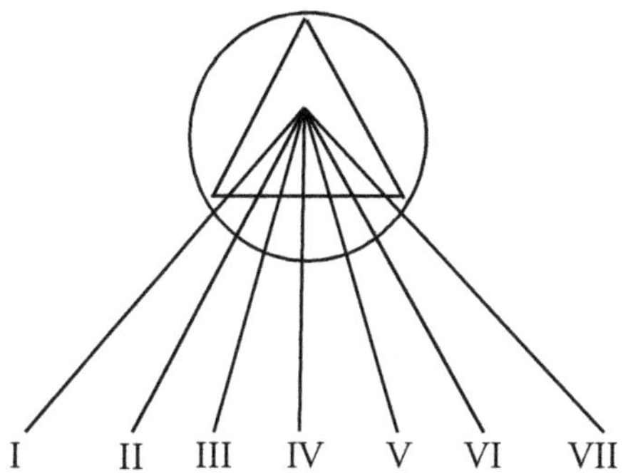

THE SEVEN RAYS OF ENERGY

This successive transmission of the Rays from one celestial objective to the next, is all based on a septenary system and on the progressive reduction in vigour of the relative energy as it is relayed from constellation to constellation, system to system or entity to entity, in ever descending order.

It must be clearly understood that the above presentation with regard to the origin of Energy from the Supreme source is merely symbolic and reflected in terms which it is hoped will provide the myopic vision of man with a picture which may throw a faint beam of light on concepts which actually lie beyond his normal comprehension. That part of the physical Universe which he can discern or record with the help of even the most sophisticated astronomical instruments only forms a negligible part of the Whole. (All such terms as the 'Whole', the 'One' or the 'Supreme Being', must be considered as purely relative or actually paradoxical when related to the concept of the Infinity of Creation, as these expressions imply demarcated boundaries or spheres of influence or being and therefore denote limitations!)

Under the circumstances it is considered futile even to attempt a more detailed description of the emblematic progress of Energy through heavenly spheres which already in themselves range beyond human comprehension. A vast intermediate phase is consequently left veiled in mystery, until the stage is reached where the student can be introduced to a rather perfunctory description of how the Divine Energy destined for our Solar System, already considerably reduced in potency in comparison with its original phenomenal power, is passed through a great triangle of Cosmic Lives consisting of the Great Bear, the Pleiades and Sirius, with the Great Bear at the apex.

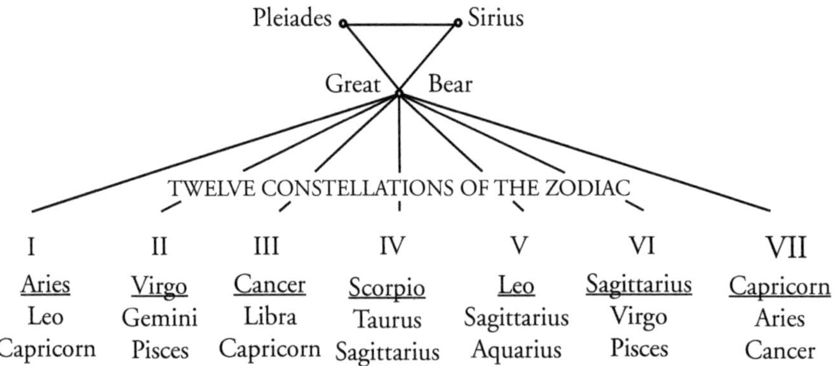

The seven Rays radiated from this Great Bear Trinity are directed through the TWELVE CONSTELLATIONS OF THE ZODIAC, which in their turn are also grouped into seven triangles from which the Rays are finally emitted and projected into space, thus reaching our Solar system as one of the seven similar systems with which ours is associated.

The Seven Zodiacal Triangles

Ray	Apex of Triangle	Base of Triangle	
I	Aries	Leo	Capricorn
II	Virgo	Gemini	Pisces
III	Cancer	Libra	Capricorn
IV	Scorpio	Taurus	Sagittarius
V	Leo	Sagittarius	Aquarius
VI	Sagittarius	Virgo	Pisces
VII	Capricorn	Aries	Cancer

The energies of these zodiacal Rays are not only radiated to the Sun, but also directly to our Solar System as a whole and therefore also to the individual planets. Actually these energies are radiated into universal Space without any bias and our Solar System is consequently by no means a specially favoured focal point of attention. Furthermore, each planet is also subjected to a wide range of other Ray influences, either relayed from our Solar Logos (through the Sun) or otherwise direct from other planetary sources or from other points of origin from the outer Cosmos.

THE SEVEN ZODIACAL TRIANGLES

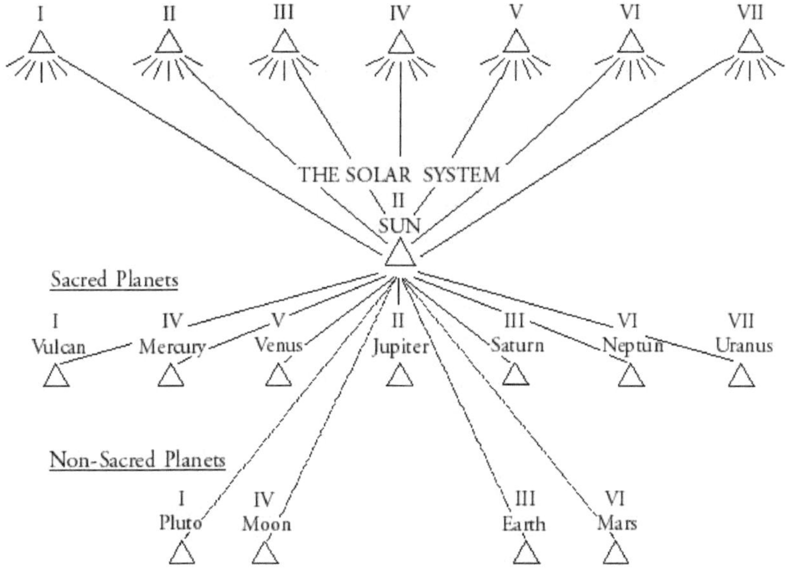

THE SOLAR SYSTEM

Sacred Planets

I	IV	V	II	III	VI	VII
Vulcan	Mercury	Venus	Jupiter	Saturn	Neptune	Uranus

Non-Sacred Planets

I	IV	III	VI
Pluto	Moon	Earth	Mars

Our planet and our solar systems have already been referred to as living entities, representing the physical reflection of our planetary and Solar Deity or Logos. In other instances certain celestial bodies have been alluded to as 'Cosmic Lives'. This is not merely a symbolic way of expression, but must be considered a matter of fact, although a concept which the uninformed may find difficult to grasp. It should be realized, however, that the underlying principle is the same as that to which the Biblical words refer where it is said that "in Him we live and move and have our being". This is actually a direct reference to the fact that each human being forms part of the Human Kingdom, which again is only one of the seven Kingdoms of Nature which in their totality compose what the average man knows as the planet Earth, which actually represents the physical expression of a living Entity in Whose body the individual human being may be regarded as functioning only as a simple atom. Relatively so few are, however, consciously aware of the fact that what man observes in physical expression merely represents the lowest of seven separate but closely integrated and interacting planes of existence, which in their totality constitute our planetary Deity, Logos, God or whatever name man may be included to attach to this Being "in Whom we live and move and have our being".

Evolutionary Scheme of our Planet

In the evolutionary scheme of our planet, composed of the seven Kingdoms of Nature, Humanity occupies an intermediate or transitional position between the spiritual and physical planes:

KINGDOM OF NATURE		PLANE
1.	Solar Lives	
2.	Planetary Lives	Spiritual
3.	Souls	
4.	Human	Transitional (dual)
5.	Animal	
6.	Vegetable	Physical
7.	Mineral	

Man is therefore actually in the process of evolving from the physical to the spiritual spheres of existence, where he will eventually take his entitled place among the countless ethereal beings functioning in their several gradations on various spiritual levels, where they are actively proceeding with their work and their responsibilities in accordance with their attained evolutionary status. At some stage or other, all these evolved Beings also passed through the phase of human existence. Because of their more highly developed state of consciousness, the conditions under which they are functioning, which seem ephemeral to us, apparently seem even more real to them than the dense material conditions to which physical man has been adapted. Yes, these are difficult concepts to understand and to accept. At any rate, to gain a clearer insight as to the position he is occupying, the student should begin by realizing that his physical body is a complex of innumerable smaller and even minute subsidiary structures or lives, all suitably co-ordinated and integrated to function as a single unit and a potentially efficient instrument under the control of the soul. On the other hand, notwithstanding deceptive appearance and lack of understanding or conscious awareness, man is again related by etheric streams of energy, not only to everything that constitutes his environment, but also to the rest of his fellow men, thus representing an integral and inseparable part of the One Humanity and the plurality of the One Planetary Life, our Logos, Who is responsible for guiding the destiny of all component parts, thus creating the many patterns through which this Life is finding expression.

Similarly, every created form is characterized by its own specific life expression, mainly differing from other forms by the degree of consciousness exhibited, which in turn provides an indication of the stage attained on the evolutionary Path of Life. Thus, man is an integrated part of the Logos of our planet Earth, Who represents a focal centre of energy in the greater Life of our Solar Logos, which again constitutes an energy centre in an even more comprehensive heavenly constellation. And Thus the pattern unfolds to reach even vaster and more indeterminate and incomprehensible dimensions!

This is merely a sketchy outline to indicate how the Divine Energy, constituting all that IS, and providing the life, character and quality to manifested form, sweeps through the Universe as a whole, serving to relate, interrelate and synthesise every created form, of whatever nature, into the One Co-ordinated Whole, the expression of the Will of the Supreme Being!

III

PLANES OF EXISTENCE

Man's Position in the Cosmic Structure

Before entering into further details about the quality and functions of the Rays, it is considered advisable that the student should be provided with some perspective of the relative position man occupies in the overall Cosmic structure, thus enabling him to recognise and to become more consciously aware of his own comparative insignificance. For this purpose only a general outline is given, indicating the several planes of existence which constitute the Universe.

According to esoteric literature, there are seven planes of Cosmic Being, of which the lowest is the Cosmic Physical Plane, which in turn comprises the seven planes of our Solar System:

	PLANE	HARBOURING
I	Divine	The solar Logos
II	Monadic	The Planetary Logoi and Human Monads
III	Spiritual	The Spiritual Will of the Triads
IV	Intuitional	The Souls of man
V	Mental	The Mental Bodies and Higher or Abstract Minds
VI	Astral	The Emotional or Astral Bodies
VII	Physical	The Physical and Etheric bodies

Each of these planes are again divided into seven subsidiary spheres or aspects, which in the case of the Physical Plane includes:

1–4	Four Etheric spheres
5	The Gaseous sphere
6	The Liquid sphere
7	The Dense Physical sphere

During the normal course of events the average man functions simultaneously on the physical plane, the emotional (astral) plane and the lower levels of the mental plane. On the physical plane, he is as a rule well acquainted with the dense, liquid and gaseous states of matter. Especially during the past century considerable progress has been achieved in harnessing and applying energies released by converting substances from one state to another. With a few exceptions, the etheric worlds still largely remain wrapped in mystery for man and it is only during recent years that science has shown an awakening interest in this relatively unknown field. The exploring of various phases of what has become known as 'extra-sensory perception' (ESP) as well as of certain aspects of 'electro-magnetism', has for instance drawn specific attention. With the gaining of experience it is expected though that these first tentative explorations will in the near future be succeeded by rapid developments.

The majority of men are to a very large extent still emotionally oriented and their lives are consequently guided by various aspects of selfish desire, the urge for satisfying sensual needs and the distorted values of the astral realms. In his evolutionary process, however, man is consistently moving towards the higher mental levels, at first instinctively, though eventually the stage will be reached when he will consciously become aware of the higher objectives of life and will deliberately strive for improved mental development and a better understanding of the meaning and purpose of existence. It is only through mental development that the hold of the emotional plane can eventually be broken and superseded, thereby allowing the Higher Mind to take over and assume control to the same extent that this process is being effected.

Constitution of the Human Personality

As already pointed out, man functions simultaneously on three of the four lower planes, namely the mental, the emotional and the physical planes. This he is enabled to do owing to the complexity of his nature. In fact, his lower being, which esoterically is known as the personality is composed of three separate although closely related bodies, which are respectively associated with the corresponding planes of existence:

1.   The Physical body, which is composed of:
      a) the dense physical aspect
      b) the intangible etheric surround, also known as the vital
          or electro-magnet aspect
2.   The Emotional or Astral Body
3.   The Mental Body

Although for the purposes of these studies reference is made to the emotional and mental 'bodies', thus leaving the impression that these aspects are present in material form, it should be explained that they merely represent vague spheres of focussed energy intimately associated with the physical body and containing the concentrated emotional and mental forces belonging to the personality, but without assuming any definite or recognisable form.

These three coherent 'bodies' constituting the personality, remain incomplete and cannot yet be regarded as representing a self-conscious human being, unless integrated, infused and controlled by the Soul that mysterious spiritual force, forming the link between spirit and matter or, in other words, between the Monad and the personality.

Diversification of Divine Energy

It has already been pointed out that all of the manifested Universe is constituted of Energy; energy evinced in its fantastic diversity, quantity and nature; energy radiated through space from its innumerable sources, streaming freely from point to point; energy impacting on the unending variety of created form, conveying and transmitting its qualities; energy being absorbed, transmuted, deflected or redirected; energy being temporarily bound and restricted into form, perhaps only momentarily or in other instances for periods stretching over aeons of time. But whatever the observed nature or the assumed character of such energy, it forever remains vibrantly alive and in a constant state of movement, notwithstanding deceptive appearances to the contrary as registered by man's limited and imperfect instruments of observation. This indestructible, all prevailing, all pervading and all encompassing energy is the Life expression of the SUPREME BEING.

The unending diversity in which this Divine Energy is manifested might for the sake of better understanding perhaps be classified into three broad categories for the purpose of the present consideration:

1. Energy temporarily commuted to form in its illimitable variety and nature, occurring on several planes of existence. This energy, depending on the assumed form and ruling circumstances, is restricted to some extent, but may nonetheless remain extremely potent or, in other circumstances, may again have been rendered relatively lethargic until triggered anew into vibrant activity.

2. The second group of energies is that composing Space or the various 'ethers', serving as a medium or vehicle for supporting, conducting, transmitting, communicating and interrelating every variety of energy, whether manifested as form or as streams or Rays. This etheric network not only surrounds every created form, but also interpenetrates it atomically. Not only does it serve as the mortar for holding together the atoms of each form, but it also serves to support such forms in their relative and required position within 'space', to interrelate and link all forms and to integrate and blend them into intermediate units and eventually into the One Whole. It is this aspect of energy which presently will be dealt with in somewhat greater detail.

3. The last group comprising the paramount theme of the present study deals with the Seven Rays of Energy which originate from the One Source, but are subsequently transmitted from point to point and from objective to objective, each Ray after impact with some specific form being split again into seven subsidiary Rays, but nonetheless ever persisting on its indicated Path through Life, proceeding in ever descending order and potency along the designated way and, in transit, serving as the creative force – transmuting, inspiring, modifying, vivifying and influencing all that is progressively contacted in fulfilment of the Divine Purpose and Plan.

Etheric System of Energy

The average man is as yet hardly aware of the existence of the vast but largely invisible and intangible etheric realms by which he is constantly surrounded; that vibrant world in which his every action, yes, even his every thought, is registered and transmitted to all that surrounds him; that vehicle through which etheric or electric waves of light, colour and sound, of energy in its multiplicity of expression, are carried to him to impact upon his personal and immediate etheric body, thus making his aware of and bringing him into contact with all that surrounds him, with the rest of the world "in which he lives and moves and has his being". For man to realise that these hidden worlds, already so difficult to visualise and understand, again occur on several planes of ever more rare, exalted or refined manifestation, can merely be accepted in theory and will only be more clearly conceived as the consciousness gradually expands and purer sensitivity is achieved.

To obtain a more distinct and comprehensible picture of the etheric complex, it is advisable to start with the atom, those minute and invisible units of creation, which when compounded in their myriads constitute the building blocks of visible matter. Today, science has become aware of the fact that these atoms are not merely microscopic and indivisible units of matter, but actually small corpuscles of focussed and concentrated energy, which may be regarded as live entities remaining in a constant state of active vibration and which by a process of 'breathing' are incessantly giving off or radiating energy to the surround, simultaneously absorbing some of the energy carried by the ether with which it is constantly being impacted.

It is only during our present 'atomic age' that science has come to the realisation of the phenomenal concentration of energy lying locked up in each separate atom. Year by year further progress is now being made in devising proper techniques for the controlled release of these pent up powers. The inherent power of energy must be regarded as a neutral force that can be applied either positively or negatively, constructively or destructively and, therefore, for good or evil. The very first use to which man applied this newly discovered force was to contrive 'atomic' weapons for the wholesale destruction of his enemies, but fortunately he is now gradually recovering some balance and is rapidly beginning to explore the innumerable avenues that are opening up to him for the beneficial use of these miraculous powers on behalf of mankind. Of recent years, considerable progress has already been made in this respect, but apparently even far more impressive and exciting discoveries are still in store for man and will be revealed to him in due course.

Returning to the subject of the etheric realms, the minute atom provides several points of correspondence with a planetary system – as above, so below! The energy in the atom is focussed in a positively charged central point or nucleus and around this symbolic 'sun' a varying number of smaller, negatively charged bodies or concentrations of energy, the so-called 'electrons', are in orbit. The actual number of these miniature 'planets' will depend on the nature of the specific atom concerned. The boundary or 'atom wall' will be determined by the orbit pattern established by the electrons, which in turn will vary in accordance with the magnetic or attractive power exerted by the nucleus.

This atom wall representing the ring-pass-not of the inner circulating energies, however, remains permeable to energies from either side of the wall, thus allowing a perpetual process of interchange of energy between the atom and its surround. The result is that each atom is moulded or shrouded in a thin layer of energy which has percolated through the wall, but which has been prevented from further escape by the magnetic power exerted by the nucleus which is holding it in close contact, thus forming a thin but completely enclosing coat of energy.

It is this surround of energy, typical of each and every atom in nature, which is known as its 'etheric or vital body'. The energy contained in this vital body is in itself of a neutral nature, mainly serving as a medium of reception, conduction and transmission for both the outgoing energies radiated from the atom, as well as for the incoming energies impacting on it from outer sources.

When smaller or larger numbers of atoms are attracted towards each other and held in congeries to form the multiplicity of structures and bodies demanded by Nature, the relative atom walls are therefore never in direct contact, always remaining separated by this thin stratum of ether, which actually simulates and in several respects fulfil the same function as a layer of mortar. On the one hand, this layer serves to retain the individuality, quality and character of the atom, but it simultaneously also provides that factor of intimate coherence which will allow these grouped atoms to resemble and act as a single co-ordinated unit. The beauty of this marvellous contrivance of nature, esoterically known as the 'etheric web', is that every form is interpenetrated down to atomic levels with an intense and all pervading etheric network, which allows for the uninterrupted and bilateral flow of energy and thus for the interrelation and communication between every single atom as well as with all of the outside world.

Because every created form is composed of innumerable atoms, each enclosed in its own etheric shroud, every composite structure will also be contained in a similar amalgamated vital body of its own, the thickness and nature of this surrounding etheric layer depending on the combined radiatory qualities of the enclosed atoms.

As already indicated, every form is composed of lesser bodies or organs and by pursuing this line of thought it can be concluded that all forms of creation are merely aggregates of atoms and therefore of focal points of energy. This same concept projected in the opposite direction, leads to the conclusion that all forms merely represent subsidiary parts of ever larger structures or entities. This consideration can be expanded to include such already comprehensive concepts as solar systems and cosmic constellations and ultimately the whole of the inconceivable Universe – the SUPREME.

All these structures, whether large or small, all these creations and concepts are actually synthesised into the One Whole by the all-encompassing Etheric system of Energy, which apart from the material world and realms revealed to man's extremely limited powers of observation and recognition, also comprises the boundless sea of energy contained in cosmic space, which in turn includes solar and planetary space and, on a still lower level, the worlds of energy in which man exists and of which he is to some extent consciously and actively aware.

Today, there is a growing recognition in scientific circles of the electro-magnetic nature of every form of creation and that every object, to a greater or less extent, radiates energy or electricity and is therefore surrounded by an electro-magnetic field, which may be either positively or negatively charged, thus serving either to repel or attract associated bodies. This electro-magnetic field is but another name for the etheric vehicle which not only surrounds and interpenetrates every manifested form, reticulated down to the most insignificant atom, but which simultaneously also serves to synthesize all of creation, including all of the sidereal worlds, into one vast Whole. It is through this immense and boundless etheric system that the One Life pours, vitalising all that IS. Narrowing this thought down to our little planet Earth, it is through our planetary etheric body, which is also pervaded and pulsating with this Divine Life, that the manifested kingdoms of Nature are vitalised and intimately related and co-ordinated with the Life currents and the variety of energies incessantly circulating through and out of every aspect of manifestation. Actually, there is no single atom of whatever nature which does not remain subject to the impact, influence and interchange of these constantly flowing and living energies, eventually serving to evolve this whole complex, constituting the physical body of our Planetary Logos, towards some unknown objective – the Divine Purpose!

IV

THE HUMAN ETHERIC BODY

The foregoing chapters led to certain considerations which as a rule are of particular interest to the average student, namely, a closer study of the subjective aspects of the human body and how and where these relate man to his environment and the overall complex. For present purposes of approach the accent is therefore not focussed on the actual physical constitution of man, but rather on his etheric vehicle, which serves a dual purpose – firstly, of integrating every part of his own physical system into a single functional unit, radiating and projecting its energies to all that comprises its surround and, secondly, of serving as the medium of reception, redirection and transmission for all incoming external energies, thus relating and integrating the individual human being not only with his immediate environment, but also with the WHOLE.

Despite the growing scientific interest in electro-therapy and the rather hesitant recognition of the role played by the etheric body, there is still, generally speaking, a deplorable lack of interest, not only in the human etheric body as such, but also in the etheric realms as a whole. The reason for this is because the majority of men are still to a large extent exclusively obsessed with their physical well-being – only living for the satisfaction of their diverse physical desires and for experiencing the ensuing emotional reactions. The consequence is that they remain bound to the astral world, unaware of the intangible realms of energy by which they are constantly surrounded, which ceaselessly impinge on their system and which, in the final instance, determine their physical condition and reactions.

The individual etheric body is primarily composed of the etheric surround of the myriads of atoms constituting the organs and physical body of the person concerned. This composite etheric field is then qualified by the energies which characterise the plane which has been attained and on which this being normally functions and reacts during his particular stage of evolution. This vital surround consists of a system of innumerable interlocking and circulating lines or streams of force, which not only interpenetrates and supports the whole physical being, but is also radiated beyond the physical form, providing it with a vibrant etheric aura, the depth, colouring and vitality of which will vary in accordance with the stage of development attained by the particular individual.

Nodal Points of Energy

Where these lines of force converge, focal points or Centres of Energy will be formed. There are numerous of these nodal points of force distributed throughout the etheric system, providing the equipment for the effective concentration and subsequent distribution of energy. The potency of these centres will vary considerably, in the first instance depending on the number of lines or streams of force concentrated in a particular centre. It is thus found that each etheric body contains:

1. Seven major centres of energy where great streams of energy converge, forming the principal stations of distribution.
2. Twenty-one second centres.
3. Forty-nine recognised smaller focal points scattered through the body.
4. Innumerable minor focal points, usually corresponding and closely related to the many nerve centres providing the physical body with its necessary sensitivity.

The final linking up between the etheric and the physical organisms is effected by the 'nadis', the name used to metaphysical studies for those minute lines and carriers of energy which interpenetrate, reticulate and permeate the physical body down to atomic levels, actually underlying the micro nervous system, which is fed, stimulated and governed by what may be regarded as its etheric counterpart. It is through the reciprocal functions between these two intimately related systems, that external impulses are transmitted to the nervous system and thence to the brain or, in the reverse order, that forces generated by the physical body, are being radiated and communicated to the etheric realm.

Seven Etheric Centres

As the main controlling stations of all energy passing through the etheric body, the seven Centres are fulfilling a most important function, as these energies are at all times responsible for the conditioning of man. It should be noted that these seven focal points of energy transmission are not located within the dense physical body, but are situated in its closely enveloping etheric surround. They nevertheless also do have their complements in the human body, as each etheric centre is not only closely related to one of the major glands in the endocrine system, but also to certain physical organs with which they are directly or indirectly associated:

THE SEVEN ETHERIC CENTRES OF ENERGY AND ASSOCIATED ENDOCRINE GLANDS AND PHYSICAL ORGANS

	Etheric Centre	Endocrine Gland	Physical Organ
1.	Head Centre	Pineal	Brain
2.	(i) Alta major	Carotid	Spinal Column
	(ii) Eye or Ajna	Pituitary	Eyes, Ears, Nose
3.	Throat	Thyroid	Vocal, Bronchial, Lungs
4.	Heart	Thymus	Heart

Diaphragm————————————————————————————

	Etheric Centre	Endocrine Gland	Physical Organ
5.	Solar Plexus	Pancreas	Liver, Stomach, Gall-Bladder
6.	Sacral	Genitals	Reproductive System
7.	Base of Spine	Adrenal	Spinal Column

LOCATION OF TWENTY-ONE SECONDARY CENTRES

Two   Just in front of the ears
Two   Immediately above the two breasts
One   Above the breast bone and associated with the thyroid gland
Two   One in the palm of each hand

Two   One in the Sole of each foot
Two   One behind each eye
Two   Associated with the genitals (male and female)
One   Associated with the liver
One   Associated with the stomach and solar plexus
Two   Closely associated with the spleen
Two   One behind each knee
One   Associated with the vagus nerve
One   Associated with the solar plexus and the base of the spine

Each of the secondary or minor energy centres occurring in the etheric body also has its counterpart reflected as unobtrusive or even unknown glands in the physical system.

The medical profession is today rapidly becoming aware of the important role played by the endocrine or ductless glands in the general maintenance of health by pouring their secreted hormones into the bloodstream, but they still remain in relative ignorance about the direct relationship between these ductless glands and their originating source of energy – the corresponding Etheric Centres.

As is the case with every other form of creation, the physical manifestation of our Planetary Logos is also qualified by an etheric surround for the reception and distribution of all aspects of the seven energies by which He is affected and these energies are also controlled in His etheric system by seven major planetary centres. Yes, as above, so below!

Seven Planetary Energy Centres

Energy Centre	Field of Expression	Controlling Ray	Nature or Objective
1. Head	Shamballa	I	Will
2. Heart	Hierarchy	II	Love
3. Throat or Ajna	Humanity	V	Intuition
4. Throat	Animal	III	Intellect
5. Solar Plexus	Vegetable	VI	Instinct
6. Sacral	Deva	VII	Responsiveness
7. Base of Spine	Mineral	IV	Synthesis

Of these seven Centres, the first three are of especial importance to man:

1. *Shamballa*: This is the seat of the "Lord of the world", supported by the "Seven Spirits before the Throne". From this Centre streams forth the Will Aspect of God, an energy which esoteric literature often refers to as the Shamballa Force.

2. *Hierarchy*: This Centre is characterised by the energy of the "Love of God" which at the present stage is swinging into one of its major cyclic approaches to Earth. One of the main functions of the Hierarchy is the right control and direction of this energy through its seven principal Ray Groups of Masters and Initiates, which again find expression through, and are supported by, forty-nine subsidiary Masters' Groups.

3. *Humanity*: Where Humanity is considered as a Centre of Energy, this refers to its etheric aspect, through which 'Divine Intelligence' comes into expression, not only on behalf of the human race, but also as a source of energy for raising the three lower kingdoms of nature to higher levels in their never ending evolutionary urge. Humanity thus serves as the macrocosm in relation to the microcosm of the lower kingdoms, thereby largely fulfilling a similar function on behalf of the subhuman kingdoms as that which the Hierarchy is performing for the human kingdom.

V

All is Relative

All that constitutes the many spheres or levels of being and of creation in general, consists of energy that remains in a perpetual state of movement. Consequently, it stands to reason that nothing resulting from the temporary concentration or cohesion of such energy at specific points in what is known to man as form or matter, is really stable. Every form of whatever nature, whether appearing to be solid, fluid, gaseous or etheric, is therefore only relatively so and actually is in a constant state of change, transition or transmutation. Nothing remains static and durable, whether an atom, a mineral or a planet. Whether noticeable to limited human perception or not, everything is in a slow or rapid process of transformation from one form of energy to another, and must therefore be regarded to be of a transitory or ephemeral nature.

All that IS, including everything observed or experienced by man, can therefore only be considered to be relative and illusory. Its nature or evaluation is dependent entirely on the time factor and point of reference from which the observation emanates. But even such a point of reference is unstable and of a fleeting nature.

Relativity alludes to the relation or association between separate phenomena, experiences, objects or concepts. It is therefore founded on comparison or appraisal of the nature and characteristics of that which is under consideration. That which is reflected in the mind of man originates to a large extent from what is registered in the brain by the five senses, either separately or jointly. The resulting image will therefore depend on the quality of the human instrument making the observation, as well as on the channels through which these are expressed. As these qualities vary to a vast degree from person to person, it may be said that when a specific object, experience or set of conditions is viewed by different observers, few will register an identical picture thereof, or feel the same reaction.

For the sake of retaining a proper perspective, the statement just made may be qualified by mentioning that the mind is not solely controlled by the physical senses. Depending on the stage of spiritual development, the soul and subtle entities providing impressions from subjective levels will play an increasingly important role in influencing and modifying the mind, thought-life and the consequent physical activities of the individual. This change in directive stimulus moving gradually from the material to the spiritual, will proceed progressively until the stage is eventually reached where the soul or rather the Monad or Spirit will take complete control, determining all bodily reactions and performances. The reactions of the individual to all outer impulses therefore remains subject or relative to his stage of development.

The concept of relativity applies to every terrain and every sphere of existence. On the one hand, it gives rise to that wonderful diversity in creation providing the variety of incentives and experiences in daily living. On the other hand, it also furnishes the grounds for innumerable human disparities and contrasts – for misunderstandings, disagreements and general discord – resulting in active conflict and never ending misery. If man could only become consciously aware of the relativity of virtually every form of matter or concept encountered during the normal course of existence, he might be led to a better understanding of life as a whole and particularly of his fellow men with their divergent viewpoints and activities. This would in turn result in greater tolerance, co-operation, compassion and, ultimately, in better human relationships.

It might therefore be useful to draw the attention more specifically to some pertinent aspects where relativity plays a distinctive role. When fully recognised as such, this might lead towards attempts at better mutual understanding which would allow life to proceed on a more even keel.

The Relativity of the Universe

No attempt will be made to formulate a description of the Universe. The intention is merely to emphasise the fact of the limitations of the human mind. Any conclusions will always remain relative and dependent upon the stage of development attained by the ever-expanding consciousness of the individual.

Theoretically the Universe is absolutely boundless and infinite, but actually these concepts are beyond the comprehension of the finite human mind. In this connection it may be remembered that only a few centuries ago, man still conceived the Earth to be the centre of all existence, with the sun, moon and stars orbiting through the heavens for the benefit of mankind. When Copernicus came to the conclusion some five hundred years ago that the Earth was in reality only a planet revolving around the sun, his theories met with violent opposition. It is, however, only during recent decades with the fantastic development of modern technology that clearer ideas have been formulated about the absolute vastness of outer space. But though this may have led the thinker to expanded horizons of awareness and consciousness, it actually has brought him no closer to an understanding of the infinite.

As an example, it may be pointed out that there is a continuously growing realisation of the vast dimensions of the galaxy of which our solar system forms such a minute part. The former is composed of billions and billions of stars, the majority of which probably constitute solar systems with only their central suns being visible to the human eye, leaving us unaware of the orbiting planets by which they are probably surrounded. How many of these conjectured planets exist and how many of them are potentially or actually habitable by human or similar beings is as yet still an open question. It is, however, quite possible that within the relatively near future improved equipment will become available which will enable the identification of at least some of these hypothetical planets. At some further stage, it may even be determined whether, and to what extent, these planets are supporting life and even something of the nature of such life.

Thus, it may eventually be found that the celestial expanses are actually teaming with life and even with beings of a similar nature as the human, though in that case probably varying in stage of evolutionary development. For the time being, these ideas remain purely speculative, providing interesting flights for imagination.

The fascination of ever deeper exploration and clearer understanding of the grandeur and nature of our galaxy and the starry heavens seems to hold never ending possibilities for the future. In recent years astronomers have determined that our galaxy is not something unique, but only one of thousands, even of billions of similar galaxies traversing as units through limitless space. Though these conceptions can be graphically worked out in the mind or illustrated on paper, they remain purely relative and the result of reducing incomprehensible dimensions to a conceivable mini-scale. During this process, the true position obviously becomes distorted losing much of its qualifying detail. Notwithstanding these limitations, just try to imagine the Master Mind required to control not only the orbiting of the illimitable planets within their endless number of solar systems, but also that of directing these vast systems grouped into larger constellations and subsequent galaxies, and all these perpetually moving through the heavens according to an orderly Plan and at the behest and Will of the ONE! Yes, though this may be an excellent mental exercise, how relatively meaningless are all the words of a limited human mind blindly groping to become aware of the immensity of it all, even though only the outermost fringes of Reality are probably being touched!

According to metaphysical or philosophical teachings, the majority of men are as yet only functioning on the physical or astral planes of existence. A smaller percentage is working on the superseding mental plane, with only relatively few attaining to the four succeeding spiritual planes. To make matters even more abstruse and incomprehensible, it is further claimed that these seven planes of existence considered as a whole only constitute the Cosmic Physical Plane or the lowest of the seven planes of the Cosmic System! By attempting to introduce these principles to the concepts of the physical Universe, which in itself already exceeds the limits of human understanding, and by trying to conceive that this physical reflection only represents the lowest aspect of several higher spiritual and cosmic planes of being, the stage is reached where these suppositions range totally beyond the capacity of the normal intellect, further accentuating the relativity of every aspect of human consciousness and experience.

The Relativity of the Concept of Deity

There are those who will regard the following thoughts as profane and reflecting disrespect towards their interpretation of the Higher Intelligence, known by so many names. Should this be the case, it will be only from lack of understanding and the incapacity to detach themselves sufficiently from preconceived notions with which they are identified. Such dogmatic tenets, acquired since early youth, prevent an unbiased approach to aspects of religious thought which, at some stage or another, are bound to crop up in the mind of every individual who is prepared to think for himself.

The principal factor by which man is distinguished from the animal is that he has been endowed with a self-conscious, reasoning and analytical mind with which he is to solve and overcome the numerous problems which confront him. It is by programming the computer-brain with the thoughts contributed by the mind that these obstructions can be surmounted. These experiences provide the lessons which enable man to advance step by step along the Path of Life. This thought-life is intended to be applied and should eventually determine every single aspect of existence with which the individual is confronted. Although the majority of men are still primarily concerned with their physical and emotional well-being, there are fortunately rapidly growing numbers who are increasingly become aware of their duality and with whom the care of the spiritual aspect of their being is of greater importance than merely attending to the needs or desires of their physical body.

There are followers of certain religions who maintain that the creeds laid down and prescribed by their particular denomination should be adhered to without question or argument, as their specific version of the Truth supplies the only way to salvation. Such a bigoted attitude cannot be accepted by any person wishing to maintain an open mind, spiritual freedom and a better understanding of the subjective worlds. If the Lord has specifically provided man with a reasoning mind, then surely he is meant to use it as effectively as possible, not only with regard to his physical and emotional needs, but also to clarify the even more important aspects of living, namely the nature of his spiritual being.

As already pointed out while expressing some thoughts on the nature of the 'Universe', our Solar System is merely a speck of dust – a minute atom in the all-embracing Universe – which represents the physical reflection of the Supreme Being. As it is, this physical aspect of the Supreme – the infinite Universe – is already far beyond all human conception and comprehension, without even bringing the various etheric or spiritual planes into consideration. It is therefore totally impossible for man to obtain even the faintest idea or image of the true essence of this Ultimate Intelligence. Thus any attempt at defining this Being must remain entirely relative and in fact merely amounts to a juggling with words.

If this is the case, since man cannot possibly form a conception of the Supreme, it is equally impossible for man to turn to this unknown, inaccessible and incomprehensible Power for help and comfort. A Power can only be invoked if it can be consciously or unconsciously visualised or conceived. By thus furnishing the relative Being with a meaningful form in the mind or imagination, this Entity immediately becomes restricted and reduced in stature to the levels attainable by the mind. That means that the essence of potency of the entity invoked by the individual will be strictly in accordance with the intellectual or the spiritual level or capacity of the aspirant and will thus be reduced to the highest spheres to which the aspirant can raise his consciousness.

When considering these ideas, the logical conclusion seems to be that if this Supreme Power lies so far beyond human ken, then the probability is that It will not have any particular reciprocal interest or even awareness of that atom in Its physical manifestation which man knows as the Solar System. How much less will this Entity be concerned with the microscopic points of energy, those insignificant little human beings passing through a transient phase of existence, which may be relatively regarded as only evolving atoms in the physical body of the Solar Atom. Yes, everything in creation is relative, all depending on the point of reference used for comparison. For the sake of argument, just consider for a moment that there are probably millions of atoms in the tip of a person's toe. The person to whose body this toe belongs is certainly not consciously aware of these teaming millions of atoms and, as long as that toe seems to be in a reasonably healthy condition, even the toe as such will hardly receive attention and will be practically ignored. Under the circumstances, is it unreasonable to suppose that a similar position may be applicable at more supernal levels of existence? As above, so below!

It stands to reason that self-opinionated man with his extremely limited field of perception, having little direct awareness of the immensity of the spheres lying beyond the confines of contact of his physical senses, will be inclined to consider himself to be playing an important role in Creation. There is no question of the fact that owing to his self-consciousness and a relatively well developed intellect, he is occupying a superior position in his immediate physical environment. Consequently, while his vision remains restricted to these narrow horizons, it is only to be expected that he should develop some degree of vanity or self-esteem, regarding himself as the elect of Creation and specially favoured by the Creator, not realising that in the greater Universe he disappears into absolute insignificance! However, by narrowing the horizons of contemplation and bringing the point of reference closer home to man and 'down to Earth', relating him with an environment with which he is more intimately acquainted and which to him is therefore more meaningful, the position assumes different proportions and values, bringing the human being into focus again and providing him with greater stature from his own point of view.

This relativity of outlook not only affects the appraisal of man's own nature and being, but inevitably influences his assessment of those enigmatic forces of which he is consciously or unconsciously aware, which are so ephemeral that they are difficult to define. They are generally referred to as Divine, originating from Deity or, more specifically, from God, Jehovah, Allah or similar designations depending on the faith concerned.

The question now arises as to what the average person has in mind when he refers to his Deity or God. To the majority, this term obviously remains extremely vague and undefined. There are those who seem to derive complete satisfaction by limiting their Deity to some symbolic form such as a stone idol or wooden effigy, which can actually be seen, touched and worshipped. Others, instead of using a material idol, try to visualise a mental image by moulding their patron in a human form, for the most part probably not even raising their consciousness above astral levels. However, no matter what their religion or approach, it seems doubtful whether two individuals will ever entertain exactly the same ideas as to what God represents to them. The outlook of each individual will be determined by his own specific physical, emotional, mental and spiritual constitution, by the extent to which the soul is in control of the personality, by the constantly varying and changing environmental conditions and circumstances where he has been placed by destiny and, finally by his sensitivity and reaction to subjective energies and influences. Furthermore as all these factors and values are in constant change during the course of a normal life covering various stages of youth, adolescence and maturity, it stands to reason that man's concepts of Deity will not remain static and will have to be adjusted or adapted from time to time in accordance with altering conditions and circumstances and with corresponding expansions of mind and consciousness.

An attempt has been made to indicate that when people refer to or worship God or the Almighty, they are in fact not referring to or invoking the Supreme Being of the Universe, which actually is far beyond mental reach. No doubt, they are truly under the impression that they are directing their petitions to the Supreme Power, not realising their own limitations and that this concept is absolutely beyond all human comprehension and supersedes any human approach or invocation.

The Power to which man so readily appeals in time of need – the highest of which he can conceive and to which he can attain at his particular stage of consciousness – probably does not exceed the spiritual Entity manifested in and controlling our Solar System, it is quite possible that man's most lofty efforts may not even find a direct response beyond our own Planetary Logos, the One Spirit of our planet. It is only fitting, however, that man in his arrogance and self-esteem, as well as in his relative ignorance, has the presumption to believe that he, in his absolute insignificance, can bring himself to the personal attention of the Supreme Being – a concept which merely remains a symbolic designation of some inconceivable ENERGY.

These thoughts are not intended to belittle man, his spiritual aspirations or the Deity he invokes for guidance and support. No, to the contrary, they are merely an attempt to gain a clearer perspective of Reality and therefore a better understanding of the relative meaning and nature of the Source of our being and of the Father to whom there is an instinctive, though oftentimes unconscious, urge or attraction. Man, as a physical personality, forms an integral part of the physical manifestation of that Entity which is commonly referred to as Nature or our physical planet Earth. Similarly, the soul of man, representing the higher or spiritual counterpart of his being which controls, synthesises and provides all the lower aspects of Life and Consciousness, may in turn be regarded as a single spark of the One Life or Spirit qualifying the Planetary Logos or that Entity which the average individual knows as God.

It is hoped that these thoughts may contribute something towards a better understanding of the relativity of the 'God' concept, which has already given rise to so much futile argument and discord between religious minded individuals and groups. These disagreements have been typical of human relationships throughout the ages and have comprised one of the main causes of endless strife and bloodshed. Because men at varying stages of development are dealing with a concept that will never lend itself to absolute definition, these contentions will persist until better understanding can be reached about the basic principles concerned. After all, what does it matter whether there are individual differences in men's ideas of the Great Unknown, once it is realised that no one can readily conceive a true, complete or adequate picture of the fullness, inclusiveness and qualities of God. The concepts which are in fact discerned or designated by individual human beings are merely personalised facets of the One Truth! Furthermore, it should be realised that all men form part of the One Life and are evolving towards the One Destiny. Something of the One Spirit is in fact reflected within each individual which will eventually be brought to expression as goodwill and loving understanding, resulting in better human relations and leading to ultimate synthesis and the One Humanity!

The Relativity of Matter and Spirit

Universal Energy, also known as 'Cosmic Atomic Matter', constitutes the basis of both Matter and Spirit. The latter are but reflections of various temporary states of energy concentration or compaction – temporary because each form, appearance or state is only relative and subject to perpetual change within the elements of space and time.

According to the Tibetan concretion of energy is in fact merely a form of illusion and the effect produced on inadequate physical senses by the interplay of various forces. This reaction is subsequently transferred via the brain to the mind and consciousness. What science refers to as atoms of matter are merely force centre or energy accretions which in point of time have reached a specific stage in evolution. As these energy units constitute the bricks from which every form of tangible matter is compounded, matter and spirit are therefore purely relative reflections of Elemental Energy. This truth is concisely expressed in the ancient esoteric adage that matter is merely spirit at its lowest point of cyclic manifestation and spirit is matter at its highest and most tenuous form of expression.

The difference between matter and spirit is therefore purely relative and based on variations in density of the energy concerned. In the physical realms of illusion in which the average man normally functions, the densest material known at present is Osmium at 22.6 gms/cc, the comparative figures for gold being 19.3 gms/cc. It is likely, however, that the molten magma of the Earth's core will eventually prove to be of a considerably higher density. According to modern astronomy, these densities are relatively insignificant when compared with that of material from what science knows as 'collapsed' or 'neutron' stars, which may apparently reach the fantastic figure of more than a billion tons in weight per cc! The relative accuracy of these claims and the means as to how this information has been established are not really relevant for present purposes. The intention is merely to convey present purposes. The intention is merely to convey the fact that regarding the density of matter, there is hardly a limit to potential variations and the bounds may exceed all understanding. Practically speaking, it may be said that there exists no limit as to the densities that are attainable and as far as human cognition is concerned, the potentialities may be considered as infinite.

On the other hand, parallel conclusions may be arrived at by studying the opposite pole to matter, namely the realms of spirit. According to esoteric teachings, life on Earth takes its course through seven planes. The lower three planes are considered to be material and are in turn superseded by four spiritual planes. These seven planes of existence are distinguished from each other by a successive decrease in density and an increase in refinement, tenuousness and spirituality as the ladder is scaled from plane to plane. Furthermore, it is taught that these seven planes in their totality constitute the lowest of seven higher 'cosmic planes'. These cosmic planes are already beyond human conception and available data provide no further details. However, to be consistent with other aspects of the unbounded Universe, it does not seem unreasonable to conclude that these cosmic spiritual planes cannot be considered as the ultimate, but that they merely represent more advanced levels leading to ever more supernal planes on the evolutionary path. Yes, even though so beyond conception, man should nonetheless make every effort to come to the realisation that every aspect of human evolution must eventually be interpreted in terms of the limitless and eternal – whatever meaning this may convey!

But let us return to less abstract and more comprehensible fields of thought – back to Earth. Metaphysically speaking, all forms in the three lower worlds of existence, that is in the physical, astral and mental spheres, are considered to consist of 'matter'. For instance, mental thought-forms have originated from spiritual energy condensed into extremely rarefied or cosmic etheric matter. Actually man's creative ability is founded on this aspect, namely his capacity to clothe ideas, emanating from spiritual spheres, in the etheric substance encountered on the abstract levels of the mental plane, thus providing them with form. By applying the proper techniques of visualisation and exercising the powers of the will for the effective direction of these energies, such thought-forms can be converted into and manifested as tangible physical substance. Therefore, relatively speaking, every form of creation is but an expression of spiritual consciousness. In its never ending variety, it may be regarded as a continuous expression of divinity directed through various instruments to be moulded and conformed in response to sensitive awareness and to the influences constituting the environment.

The One Life when manifested in the objective worlds first gives rise to the duality of matter and spirit which, however, gradually disappears during the process of evolution as the element of form is progressively transcended to attain spiritual levels, thereby losing its material qualities while being re-absorbed into spirit. While life is still expressed in form, the following are some of the dualities which may be distinguished:

Spirit	and	Matter
Father	"	Mother
Life	"	Appearance
Positive	"	Negative
Light	"	Darkness
Good	"	Evil

By following another approach, it may be said that the interplay between the Father (Spirit) and the Mother (Matter) aspects will eventually result in the appearance of the Son or Consciousness aspect. It is this latter principle which provides all matter with divine Life and the diversity of form and consciousness. Therefore, all that is manifested is founded on the triplicity of FATHER-SON-MOTHER, which may also be expressed as Spirit-Consciousness-Matter, Spirit-Soul-Body or as Life-Quality-Appearance.

Matter, in its primordial state of energy, is not possessed of consciousness, because this factor only emerges as the product of interaction between Spirit and Matter. Only when these two aspects are blended in the course of creation and evolution will the fusing result in sentient response, in the many variations and degrees of consciousness and, finally, in the generation and radiation of 'Light'. In the human being this interaction between Spirit and Matter gives rise to the Soul and man's stage of evolution will be reflected by the brilliancy of the light emitted from this inner being.

VI

THE RELATIVITY OF KNOWLEDGE

Part of the cosmic energy of Light proceeding on its way through the ethers of the Universe is in due course also directed through the micro-cosmos of human existence occurring on that insignificant little planet Earth. To the average human being, however, with his extremely restricted perspective, this little world in which he finds himself remains all important and he is hardly even conscious of the presence of other realms of existence beyond the confines of the physical world as known through his five senses.

Each individual finds himself on his own particular Path of Development, gradually but increasingly becoming aware of the subjective realms by which he is surrounded. Actually, this is an extremely slow and dreary process, spread over an innumerable range of lives. It is this progressive recognition of the true nature of being in ever expanding horizons of consciousness which is commonly known as knowledge and subsequently, after maturing, as wisdom. It is often claimed that such knowledge is based on facts, but the time will come when it will be realised that even all so-called 'scientific facts' are merely relative concepts subject to change and to different interpretation with the further expansion of consciousness.

In man's daily struggle for existence there is a constant striving to acquire more and better knowledge about the many facets and spheres of life. As a rule, his primary objective is to improve and better qualify himself for the demands of life, thus enabling him to gain some advantage over competitors for anticipated rewards, whether of material or emotional nature. It will in fact take the experience of many lives before the individual gradually gains sufficient wisdom to realise that though the acquiring of ever more knowledge is certainly of considerable importance, the underlying motive should be altruistic and not the achieving of superiority over rival candidates. Man's purpose should therefore be to qualify himself to reach his highest potential with the equipment at his disposal under the circumstances where he finds himself. Then, with dedicated efforts, he should try to serve as an effective instrument for promoting the interests of his fellow men and of humanity in general.

Wisdom is progressively attained by extracting the true essence from knowledge and both knowledge and wisdom are in turn merely aspects of Truth. All these aspects of Light remain entirely relative, though steadily gaining in stature with acquired experience and the corresponding expansion of consciousness. But whether these various phases of consciousness are described as Knowledge, Understanding, Wisdom, Intuition or Truth, as concepts they remain vague and indeterminate definitions and are therefore purely relative, depending largely on the development of the aspirant and his approach to life.

The Nature of Knowledge

It is by means of the five senses that man first learns to recognise and then to experience the material aspects of Life. These sensations are subsequently transmitted to and recorded in the brain, that wonderful computer of which man disposes, in which the multiple facets of daily life are processed, correlated and converted for eventual redefinition by the mind or intellect. But apart from the perceptible and emotional experiences, knowledge is also acquired through mental channels, which may again be effected by mental experience, by specific studies or by the unconscious absorption through the mind and the subsequent processing of knowledge by the built-in computer.

The material progress of humanity is founded on the practical application of knowledge in daily living, which progressively finds expression in the arts and sciences. The latter provides the medium for the discovery and recognition of ever fresh aspects of knowledge derived either from the manipulation of facts from the existing vast store of accumulated knowledge or from that inexhaustible but as yet relatively unrealised source – "the raincloud of knowable things".

Knowledge is that energy which in the case of the average person is primarily concerned with the material aspects of evolution. As such, it represents the distorted reflection on physical, emotional and mental levels of human perception of that which already exists in far more rarefied and intangible forms on more supernal levels. It is therefore an entirely relative concept. Its quality depends on the state of development of the instrument concerned and its sensitivity, receptivity and reactivity to that which is available in subjective spheres to which the instrument must first be suitably attuned before recognition and identification can be effected.

Furthermore, knowledge is composed of a wide range of factors, each again having several facets and interpretations, the more subjective aspects stretching far beyond the scope of consciousness of the majority of men. Therefore, although the knowledge of the average individual is principally concerned with the objective side of experience, those who are somewhat more advanced will become involved with the application of energies and forces rather than with the mere study of the form that is being energised. Before this can be effected, however, the faculty for the proper perception of and identification with the more ephemeral aspects of existence must be developed and firmly established. This in turn will unfold the capacity to attain consciousness on certain spiritual planes, thereby allowing the recognition of an ever expanding field of Truths.

Therefore, the type or nature of knowledge being dealt with by the individual depends entirely on the level of consciousness achieved and the extent to which the art of effectively manipulating energies and forces has been acquired. These energies in their multiplicity of quality have their origin in innumerable sources. Though man's efforts commence on the three material levels of human endeavour, with gained experience and progressive evolution, they will eventually include successful operations on spiritual spheres.

The theme of knowledge may be further dealt with under three broad classifications. First, there is what might be called theoretical knowledge, where such knowledge is based on the findings of others who are supposed to speak with authority regarding a specific subject or field of investigation. Under the circumstances, such information is accepted without further verification by the average, untrained person.

Secondly, there is what may be described as discriminative knowledge, where the analytical and the reasoning mind is brought into play with the relative facts carefully weighed, considered and subjected to discrimination in accordance with the qualifications and competence of the investigator. This is the procedure generally followed during scientific investigations, in the course of which those factors not scientifically justified are discarded. It is because of this approach that scientists as a rule are slow and hesitant in acknowledging or accepting esoteric principles, which to them are far too intangible and of a nature that cannot be established by direct weighing or measurement.

Finally, we may speak of intuitive knowledge, which is not based on objective or scientific facts, but relates to information that has been inspired from spiritual levels and emanates from the "raincloud" of ideas. This intuitive information or instruction is always at man's disposal, but cannot be contacted, recognised and adequately applied until the necessary sensitivity and perceptivity of mind has been developed.

It is commonly assumed that knowledge refers to accumulated factual information. Furthermore, it is generally not realised that man also has access to a form of instinctive knowledge extracted and stored by the soul from experiences in previous incarnations, which has somehow been retained and projected into the realms of memory of the present life. There are occasional instances where individuals have actually recovered conscious recollection of experiences gained during past lives.

The aspirant should always keep in mind that to attain to spiritual levels, he must first pass through the higher mental levels, for which purpose the gaining of certain aspects of knowledge is essential. Therefore, the transition to supernal spheres can only be effected when the functions of the Heart and the Head are co-ordinated, in other words, when the Path of Light becomes identified with the Path of Love and thus synthesised into the Path of Life. To generalise, it might be said that the esotericist primarily follows the path of Knowledge and the mystic that of Love. However, to reach their final destination, these two paths have to converge and become integrated as the path of Spirit or Life. Again, this accentuates the relativity of knowledge which, in its ultimate perspective, is but the intelligent expression of Love or the blending of the higher mind with devotion.

During the process of maturation, every young person has to acquire a great deal of knowledge over a vast field of experience in preparation for the many demands of life. Furthermore, it should be realised that this process of learning and gathering the many facts of life is never ending. It begins from the day of birth and only ends for that particular incarnation when the soul is released and enabled to garner the essence from the experiences and knowledge gained during its temporary occupation of the physical vehicle. Each individual is incarnated with a definite purpose, to gain particular experiences and learn lessons in the course of that specific life. To ensure that the maximum advantage will be secured from these experiences, it is of the utmost importance that the person concerned be prepared as adequately as possible by acquiring all the relative knowledge that may be available.

The aspirant should understand that the securing of knowledge and experience will always demand some form of payment or sacrifice. Nothing worthwhile is ever attained in life without making some commensurate and compensatory contribution in order to restore the balance of the expended energies. But eventually these same laws will also yield their positive results, leading to expansion of consciousness and spiritual unfoldment corresponding with the nature of the transmuted inner knowledge.

Knowledge is the intelligent reward of experiment and experience. At first, it often leads to pain and distress, but eventually results in the acquiring of more dependable information and the recognition of deeper verities which can be stored for future application. This serves to prepare the aspirant for the ever growing demands and responsibilities of evolutionary existence and generates ever clearer Light and vision.

All education is thus primarily based on the principle of systematically, yet discriminately, equipping the child with suitable knowledge in preparing him for fulfilling his destined role as a constructive member of his community.

Modern civilisation is largely founded on knowledge acquired in respect of an expanding field of scientific investigation. This forms part of the systematic evolution of the human intellect and inclination to move on to the mental plane. As with all else, accumulating and advancing knowledge can be applied either beneficially or detrimentally to human interests, the effect largely depending on whether the instrument through which such knowledge is being channelled is selfishly or altruistically oriented. As a matter of course, increased knowledge and a developing intellect will inevitably result in a clearer appreciation and understanding of man's own nature, constitution and being. Step by step this will also lead to a better conception of the meaning and purpose of life and recognition of and identification with the path that should be followed. In this connection, it should always be remembered that the knowledge acquired by any individual, coming from whatever source, will primarily depend on his own approach and the dedication and persistence of his efforts. But at the same time, knowledge entails certain obligations as well as responsibilities and when such deeper discernment is provided, it should be used constructively in everyday life to the benefit of fellow men.

As the aspirant thus advances long the Path of Life, the soul begins to exert an ever growing influence over the personality, resulting in corresponding mental co-ordination. This will be achieved as a result of a clearer perception, recognition, interpretation and finally identification with the sources of information perpetually available on supernal levels, as well as from the more effective transmission of such enlightenment from the mind to the physical brain resulting in more distinctive and truer reflection of the relative facts.

Knowledge is therefore a most elastic and relative concept. Even the best equipped human intellect can absorb and utilise merely a fraction of the inexhaustible supply of that which is available to man. In practice, it will be found that it is often more effective to know just where and how needed information may be found and extracted, rather than to clutter up the computer with masses of irrelevant facts which may never be put to use during the present life. The same principle apparently is also applicable to those functioning in spiritual realms.

Therefore, it lies beyond the capacity of the ordinary human being to gather and co-ordinate all available knowledge in its present day profusion and innumerable ramifications. As far as the esoteric student is concerned, all that is expected of him is a reasonable acquaintance with the fundamental principles of life and being and sufficient knowledge to provide him with the needed Light for distinguishing his own Path. Such Light must in turn be shared with others, thus not only serving as a contribution for illuminating the path of his neighbour, but also that of the human race as a whole. Each individual is therefore endowed with his own particular Light in accordance with his destiny, place and circumstances. Such gifts and faculties, however, are not bestowed solely for personal development or selfish purposes, but to be shared with the rest of humanity for which he forms an intrinsic part. It should be clearly realised that once man has entered the Path of Return, any undue retention of gained knowledge for exclusive personal use will inevitably lead to some form of stagnation or disease in the physical body or to emotional and mental frustration. Proper assimilation can therefore only be achieved provided efforts are made to pass on all useful information for the benefit of fellow strivers and for a needy world in general.

Understanding

During the earlier stages of man's development, knowledge is mainly applied for selfish purposes and the promotion of material well-being. For each individual the time will come when the soul gradually gains control, providing him with a clearer perspective and deeper understanding of the purpose of life. The material aspects will then become identified with spiritual issues, thus resulting in the expression of wisdom. Understanding must therefore be regarded as the catalyst needed for transmuting material enlightenment into wisdom.

When considering understanding, we are again dealing with a most relative concept which depends upon the level of approach. On the material levels of daily experience, understanding entails the drawing of logical conclusions from presented facts. When thoughts are directed towards higher realms, towards the life of spirit, then understanding become the forerunner or sine qua non of Revelation, without which there can be no real expansion of spiritual consciousness.

Before there can be true understanding of the problems of others, deep insight and recognition must first be acquired of one's own character and those factors which effect man's well-being and motivate personal thought and activity. It is only after these elements have been made in controlling and regulating these influences within one's own personality that genuine understanding of the problems of fellow men can be achieved. So often it will be found that fixed theories, ideals and beliefs, largely founded on self interest, will obscure the vision to such extent that there remains no possibility of forming an unbiased estimation or apprehension of the dilemmas with which others have to contend. Such mental obstruction as a rule is the product of selfishness supported by associated characteristics of self esteem, stubbornness and separative superiority. These negative attitudes can never result in impartial evaluation and discrimination and can only be checked by introducing an inflow of the energy of pure Love. Where such Love is brought into play, the barricades of harshness, cruelty, discord and dissension and their evasion of the truth will step by step be demolished and superseded by a spirit of goodwill and loving understanding.

What a wonderful experience it is once a clearer perspective is gained of the workings of the inner man, providing a glimpse into the subjective motivations giving rise to thought and ensuing activities. How marvellous to have a conception of the incentives underlying the attitudes and performances of others. Though this may not mean approval, it will certainly result in better understanding rather than indiscriminate and harsh criticism or condemnation. What a difference it makes to life once even a faint understanding is gained of the divine Plan and Purpose, with the first rays of supernal Light illumining the path towards a dimly discernable Objective.

Fellow strugglers can be considerably encouraged in their upward striving if understanding is shown of their efforts. With such support, even apparent or temporary failures may often be changed to success. Loving understanding will lead to a true appreciation of both the motives and actions of friends and associates, to a recognition of their shortcomings and a prizing and cherishing of their virtues.

In the case of children the value of loving understanding cannot be sufficiently stressed. As yet, there are relatively but few parents or teachers who have reached the stage of truly understanding the young ones for whom they are responsible, because they themselves know so little about the functioning of the mind and the inner realities of life. In practice, so few take the trouble of explaining to their children or pupils the underlying reasons for their actions and what exactly they are trying to achieve, not realising that such explanations will inevitably produce a positive response. This understanding must therefore be reciprocal, with the person in charge having a thorough insight and appreciation of the mentality of the child and with the latter realising what his senior has in mind.

The emphasis should definitely not be on the numerous or petty little errors or misdeeds of the child, which quite often should simply be ignored, even though these supposed offences may prove rather annoying to the set ways and opinions of the teacher or parent. Those offences which should receive attention are infringements on the rights of others and the disadvantages of negative attitudes such as hate, revenge, greed and other forms of selfishness should be stressed. The child requires firm discipline, but it should be the discipline of love, persistently and sympathetically expressed as loving understanding, imposed on the children with never ending patience and careful explanation. The right approach should engender trust in the teachers, induce a sense of security in the children and dissipate fear with the realisation that the good in life can be achieved through love. Yes, without doubt a difficult and demanding task, but a task that should prove most rewarding and is assured of success when approached with dedication.

There is a natural Law of Understanding slowly permeating racial consciousness which will receive increased expression as an awareness of the brotherhood of man is established. With this comes a growing realisation that all souls are in fact identified with the One Oversoul and that our entire system is animated and integrated by the One Life with its primary attribute of Love. According to the Tibetan, this Law of Understanding will receive special attention and impetus during the Aquarian Age now being entered which will eventually lead to a world-wide spirit of greater tolerance, understanding and finally to a general recognition of spiritual realities.

True understanding can only be achieved through the ability to redirect the focal point of living from the form life to the realms of spirit. The problem is, however, that while the aspirant is functioning in the material world of men, such withdrawal must be executed with discrimination and the avoidance of any tendencies towards or leaving the impression of isolation or superiority. In practice, real understanding involves the capacity of loving identification and participation in the problems of others and loving all beings, while retaining a degree of personal detachment, thereby avoiding undue emotional entanglement. It therefore requires a sympathetic and inclusive appreciation of the life and needs of those to be helped, whilst simultaneously negating all those qualities which erect barriers or give rise to criticism and strained relations. Understanding is therefore identifying the love of the soul with the needs and demands of the form.

In this world of ours love, goodwill and understanding walk hand in hand, providing the only practical and infallible way to improved human relationships and eventual world peace. These attributes are in fact the essentials required to achieve identification with any form of divine expression. It is only with the help of these divine energies that right relations will ever be attained in the turbulent world of men, for there can be no true spiritual understanding without that most vital factor – the energy of LOVE.

Wisdom

Whereas knowledge is largely concerned with reactions emanating from the form with its material aspects, wisdom in the first instance is related to that which is subjective or spiritual, reflecting the unfoldment of the energies of Life within the progressively changing vehicles of form. Wisdom is closely involved with the essence of things, which in man is represented as expansions of consciousness. It will also be found that the aspirant is no longer guided along the Way purely by his reasoning faculty, but that the latter is gradually being superseded by a deeper understanding and subsequent intuitive apprehension of the values of life. This allows for a clearer distinction of realities and the ability to discriminate between the false and the true, the spurious and the genuine. Wisdom is thus responsible for a more intimate blending and harmonising of true values on the Path of Realisation.

Another way of expressing this is to define wisdom as the implementation in daily living of all knowledge gained by experience and perception, after subjecting such knowledge to steadfast Love. This process will ultimately find expression in service of a nature corresponding with the position achieved on the Path of Return.

In connection with this reference to Love, it must again be stressed that Love in its purest form is not sensual or emotional. It is a supernal energy which can be clearly conceived only by the spiritual man who is mentally focussed. For the effective direction of the energy of Love, a close identification is essential between the activities of both head and heart. Once these functions are firmly established and properly co-ordinated, an ever increasing Light will be germinated, serving to illuminate the path to be followed.

The human being, in response to contact with the energy of Love, gains understanding, leading to identification, inclusiveness and synthesis with other forms of creation within the environment. Wisdom is energy in action, denoted the skill or ability with which this Light of Understanding can be focussed, merged and blended with the point of need, thus leading to a specific act of service which will be determined by the inherent characteristics or inclinations (Ray influences) of the channel through which these energies are being expressed.

The majority of men are still living in a world of glamour, their minds shrouded in astral mists which distort the image of all that is sensed, observed and experienced. The only adequate way of dispelling this glamour is by subjecting it to the energy and light of wisdom. It is by means of the Light and Love of the Soul that man progressively converts his practical knowledge into wisdom. However, true wisdom will not be achieved until the grip of matter has been shaken off completely, which means attaining to the ranks of the Masters.

The Masters function primarily on the mental plane in etheric bodies, one of their principal tasks being to impress thoughts and ideas upon the minds of those human beings who are sufficiently advanced to be sensitive and receptive to such inspiration and guidance. Although in certain instances these impressions are consciously received by workers, generally, the individuals concerned remain totally unaware of the source of such impression, regarding this superior knowledge as an inspiration from their own bright intellect.

It must certainly not be assumed that wisdom is acquired solely by accumulating a vast store of knowledge during the present phase of existence. On the contrary, it is often surprising what words of wisdom may be expressed by immature youngsters or by persons who according to usual human standards are considered relatively uneducated. Such words of wisdom are actually the expressions of an "old soul" who has brought over into the present incarnation the essence of a vast range of experience garnered during numerous previous lives.

Whereas knowledge deals with so-called facts and experiences encountered during the material living, wisdom relates to the essence gleaned from such knowledge after it has been exposed to spiritual influences as the Light and Love of the Soul. Wisdom is therefore not of a factual nature, but must be regarded as a sublimation of the intellect and of inspiration and impulses which, when correctly interpreted and applied, will contribute towards both individual and general progress. It therefore represents deeper understanding, the grasping of the subjective meaning of the presented facts and, subsequently, the correct application of conclusions reached to current problems. However, all these factors can only be brought to practical expression, and applied in service of man, when they are fused, blended and motivated by the energy of Love.

Thus, it is the experiencing soul that is integrating and co-ordinating all gained factual knowledge, which by introducing the time factor into the evolutionary pattern, is developing new values and understanding of the nature and purpose of being. It is this progressive discernment that eventually gives rise to an improved sense of proportion and an inner sense of synthesis which are then translated and expressed as wisdom. Wisdom therefore is the expression of the creative power of the soul assimilating and transmuting the many facets of material knowledge in accordance with the factor of time, thus providing a clearer reflection of the Light and serving to reveal something of the world of meaning of which the phenomenal form is but the distorted reflection. Nonetheless, even wisdom must be regarded as merely a superior version of knowledge, as it still remains only a relative aspect or reflection of the all inclusive supernal TRUTH!

VII

Nothing in Life Remains Stable

If the average person is questioned as to his primary objective in life, then there are many thoughtful people whose reaction is to state that they are striving for 'stability', probably without realising the many implications and therefore the relativity of this term. The underlying meanings of the word 'stability' contain much which on closer analysis must be considered somewhat paradoxical. Thus certain concepts must definitely be considered highly commendable, as for instance such aspects of stability as constancy, dependability, security, trustworthiness, steadfastness, strength and firmness. On the other hand, there are other nuances of meaning contained in this word, such as remaining static, stationary, invariable or unchangeable, which must be regarded as of doubtful merit or in some respects even undesirable or unfeasible, because life never comes to a standstill and actually remains one long and perpetual process of change – of constant adaptation, building, breaking down and reconstruction, affording "no peace for the wicked".

Perfect stability is therefore, when literally considered, an absurdity leading inevitably to stagnation and death. But even what is commonly known as 'death' is strictly speaking no final or stable condition. Death is merely indicative of the end of some specific phase, or entry into another stage of that constant and never ending process of the flow of energy, of integration and disintegration, of synthesis and dissolution, of growth and decay and of mobilising and disbanding, to which all forms of life and matter are for ever subjected. This holds true whether we are dealing with an atom, with man or a planet.

Life Means Constant Change

During a single span of life physical man is born, grows up through successive juvenile stages and reaches maturity (which is a most relative concept), only to enter a period of physical decline which inevitably leads to 'death' of the human vehicle. Therefore individual or personality life, like all else, remains in a constant state of change, never coming to a standstill, because man is either growing and developing or he is beginning to decline and degenerate. But these processes are as a rule not very clear cut because we are dealing with the intricacies of the constitution of man and therefore are confronted with the simultaneous development of three separate bodies, namely the physical or vital body, the emotional or astral body and the mental body, all three closely related and interacting in what is known as the personality, but each nonetheless evolving at its own rate and each subject to its own specific range of activating energies. Yes, what a complicated muddle! Just try to imagine the task with which the soul is confronted to supervise and co-ordinate the gradual integration of these separate aspects which in the average man still remain in a state of chaos and which must be marshalled into a well organised and integrated 'personality' to serve the soul as an efficient instrument for the gaining of experience.

The problem arises that so often the development of the various aspects of the human personality does not follow a parallel, fixed or even course, for one aspect may be unfolding far more rapidly than another or, what so commonly occurs is that whilst the physical body may already show signs of degeneration, the mental body has not yet nearly reached its prime and may actually keep on developing till well advanced middle-age or sometimes even till after reaching relative old-age. What is so interesting about this subject is that no two individuals will ever follow exactly the same pattern and also that the tenor of change in a single life always remains unpredictable, sometimes being disappointing and in other instances soaring to unexpected climaxes.

The Evolution of the Soul

The above remarks primarily concern changes in the personality, but the most significant transitions effected are surely those of the spirit, which over the aeons have quietly been taking their course. And this is where the attention must again be focussed on the duality of man. The aspect of man that really matters is not the phenomenal and transient personality so evident to the senses, but the inner 'immortal' guiding spirit, the intangible soul, only availing itself of the personality for acquiring experience in the world of matter. In the Ancient Wisdom studies it is taught that the soul makes its initial appearance as a spark of the One Spirit with which animal-man is endowed providing him with 'self'-consciousness, thereby 'individualising' him in the process raising him from the animal to the human kingdom. It is this spark of consciousness, this minute spiritual entity, which is withdrawn from the physical body at the end of each span of life, only to be reincarnated over and over again after longer or shorter periods of abode in the realms of spirit, each time entering a new young body and thus repeating the procedure of experiencing life in the phenomenal world. Each of these successive incarnations takes place under a fresh range of circumstances, thus providing ever novel experiences which in their totality ensure the gradual evolution of the soul.

Although mention has been made of the 'immortal' nature of the soul, this term in the present instance may be regarded as somewhat ambiguous, because when after innumerable reincarnations over the course of millennia the soul has gradually evolved to relative 'perfection', it will be absorbed or assimilated by the Monad or Spiritual Triad to continue its evolution in the realms of Spirit with no further need for temporal or mortal experience.

As far as the concrete human mind can conceive these supernal concepts, this evolution of divine Entities will steadily proceed on spiritual planes, achieving ever higher and higher spiritual stature, but never coming to a conclusion or reaching a final objective and 'stability', merely serving as stations along the Way for momentary reorientation before proceeding further on the never end Path of Light.

The Golden Mean

The aspect of stability which the unsettled and confused aspirant is looking for, is really that of balance, trying to find the 'middle way' which may be followed through a world of extremes, thus avoiding being swept away by the unstable currents of emotion which so often end in various forms of fanaticism. Such equilibrium will only be found by gaining emotional control, which can be achieved by overcoming the glamours of the astral world by means of the light provided by the mind and inspiration of the soul. In due course and after acquiring the necessary experience, this will lead to wisdom and a truly wholesome and integrated personality, qualified by a proper sense of proportion and sound values, and brought into effective expression by discrimination.

Stability also denotes steadfastness and the capacity to stand as a safe and firm fortress at the centre of surrounding human contention and ever changing circumstances. This therefore implies equipoise and strength in readiness for action. As point out, such serenity and fortitude can only be achieved after the disturbing influences of the emotions have successfully been superseded by the clear light and guidance of the soul.

In times of stress the disciple often finds it difficult to preserve correct sense of proportion and to turn his activities in the right direction, which should consist of a well balanced expressed of the dictates of the soul suitably correlated with the outer needs of man as determined by the normal demands of life. To maintain this balance sounds simple enough, but so many fail to do so. Some obtain a fleeting glimpse of the Path of Light, but before they manage to establish a firm footing on this ephemeral Way, they are pulled back only to succumb anew to the overwhelming attractions of the astral life of desire and unappeased emotions. Having once again been plunged into a fresh vortex of sensual living, it may take considerable time and consecrated effort before such an individual will again attend to the insistent inner voice. And the, encountered on the other extreme, are those who having vaguely become aware of a light ahead, but not yet clearly distinguishing its nature and while still partly under the distorting influence of the astral world, are inclined to rush forward blindly and fanatically in their unbalanced enthusiasm. This happens because they still allow themselves to be guided by their emotions instead of their minds. These fanatics not only retard their own progress but may also exercise a harmful influence on those who look to them for guidance. Such lack of balance is therefore a most concrete danger that has already been responsible for the temporary downfall or at least serious delay of numerous over-enthusiastic but still unprepared aspirants.

The disciple on the Path must therefore be ready to accept ever changing world conditions and to adapt himself accordingly. He should also be prepared to contribute his fair share towards the circulation and redirection of the fresh energies which are now pouring in from supernal spheres for the promotion, acceleration and consummation of new and unequivocal changes in the evolutionary pattern of humanity which is now rapidly taking shape and which is heralding the Aquarian Age!

TRUTH

The Endless Quest

Over the ages man has consistently, either consciously or unconsciously, been in search of the Truth. This search will never be consummated. On the contrary, it will be perpetuated from generation to generation until the end of human time or, in other words, until the ever evolving human race has fulfilled its destiny according to Divine Purpose and Plan. Even when the human standards, that is after its cyclic reincarnation into physical existence has been terminated and evolution is proceeding in supernal spheres, this search for clearer perception and definition of the Truth will apparently still persist. This eternal quest remains the basis of spiritual evolution on the ever ascending and ever expanding Path of Light, leading back to the Father's House and perhaps even beyond to some indeterminate cosmic destiny.

During the earlier stages of man's development (and even today in the case of the majority of human beings) this search has been largely unconscious. As a rule, it is brought into expression as instinctive yearning, aspiration or even worship of hidden or unknown powers. Such belief in subjective powers usually arises from or is stimulated by racial tradition, however, in many instances it may result from some form of direct psychic contact with the astral worlds. This awareness that man's existence and the course of events are somehow influenced by hidden forces or invisible, intangible entities, may logically arouse a sense of apprehension or fear, which in turn may tend towards the introduction of various forms of appeasement or propitiation of these obscure forces. This actually constitutes the basis of many primitive religions which, influenced by a variety of ever changing circumstances and conditions, leads to innumerable beliefs, superstitions and traditions. However primitive and even ridiculous some of these ancient devotional practices might appear to the modern observer, they were all undoubtedly founded on some version or inkling of the Truth. Furthermore, it is logical to suppose that if more evolved entities from higher spheres were to contemplate the religious views, attitudes and practices of the average human being of today, these beliefs or practices would probably appear to them equally primitive.

What is Truth?

No true definition can be made of the Absolute Truth, because this is something beyond all human and even super-human conception. Probably the closest approach to such a definition would be to state that Truth may be regarded as being an integral and inalienable part of the Supreme Being. In terms of this, Truth must then also be regarded as a primary and Divine Energy by means of which the Ultimate is manifested throughout the infinite Universe.

Because of man's extremely limited faculties, referring not only to his senses but also to his mind or intellect, that which the average person generally registers is merely the physical manifestation. This physical world of which he is consciously aware is only the lowest of seven planes which constitute our solar system. It is first of all superseded by the Astral plane and then successively by the Mental plane and by four Spiritual planes. Collectively, these seven planes in turn represent the Cosmic Physical plane, the lowest of seven supervening Cosmic planes of existence.

Yes, when dealing with these concepts, one involuntarily comes to the realisation that words are really so extremely limited, so crude and so futile for expressing these subjective verities. And as a matter of fact, so is the mind, although at times the mind does undertake flights of perception which may far transcend the field of verbal expression. Relative to the animal world, man certainly has been granted a great privilege to be endowed with a self-conscious and reasoning mind, as well as with the faculty of expressing his thoughts quite effectively in words. But what an advancement it will be when we have evolved to the state where we may communicate with our fellow men directly from mind to mind on mental and even spiritual levels, without the restriction of first having to reduce these thoughts into words, thereby already distorting them, and providing false perspectives of the emanating thoughts and warping the concept of the Truth as perceived by that particular mind. While considering this aspect, it must however be acknowledged that there are certain individuals who are far more proficient in expressing themselves in words than others.

But let us revert to our main theme and to ever more words, as the latter for the present remain our most effective medium of intelligent communication.

Absolute Truth is Beyond Human Conception

As pointed out above, the Absolute Truth is an intrinsic expression of the Supreme Being and is therefore totally beyond all human conception. This Virginal Truth apparently is beamed into the Universe as Seven Rays of Energy, each of these Rays being qualified predominantly by certain specific aspects of the Absolute Truth. The original potencies of these Rays must be super-phenomenal and nothing on the level of human existence would be able to withstand their force. However, these Rays are in the first instance directed towards Cosmic Entities, Bodies or Constellations specially adapted for the conversion or reduction of these Energies. In the process of passing through these Entities, each Ray is split up into seven subsidiary Rays of lesser potency before moving on to their next objective. How often this process of successive septennial sub-division is repeated in the cosmic spheres is unknown. What concerns us as human beings is that these Energies, purveying Divine Truths, finally reach the Earth via the seven 'sacred' planets of our solar system, in potencies that can be effectively absorbed and controlled by the Lord of the World. These forces are subsequently directed through Shamballa to the Hierarchy of Masters who, in their turn, are responsible for their reticulation to Humanity and the lower kingdoms of nature. (See the relative diagrams on pages **38 and 39**).

At this stage, it may be pointed out that these Energies, as they are systematically reduced in power from their SOURCE to the planes presently occupied by man, are not only reduced in potency by each successive step, but are simultaneously curtailed in the expression of the purity or quality of the embodied Truth. This inadequate attempt at expressing these processes should not be misunderstood, for notwithstanding the lowering in potency of the Truth, the strength of these forces are still so powerful when reaching our Deity that they must be considerably abated while being passed through Shamballa for the benefit of the Hierarchy and Humanity. It is, however, when these Truths are being brought down to human levels and have to pass through the surrounding Astral plane that they really become subject to distortion. In this connection it must be noted that every form of energy has both its positive and negative aspects, the effect of its application depending upon which aspect is brought into expression as a result of predominating circumstances, the quality of the instruments manipulating these forces and the nature of the bodies on which the energies are acting.

The Deceptive Astral Plane

The 'watery' Astral plane is a sphere of glamour, deception, misrepresentation and illusion. Therefore, it is no wonder that the average man, for the most part still moving in this world of emotion – of innumerable interacting forces, urges and desires – obtains a badly warped or even negative impression of the Truth. It is only during the course of aeons that man develops and improves his mental capacities, thereby gradually learning to penetrate and dissipate the astral mists, thus step by step gaining a clearer view of the Truth.

Relativity of Truth

The relativity of all Truth as revealed to the myopic vision of man, must always be kept in mind. As knowledge, understanding, wisdom and consciousness expand, it will be discovered that the Truths of today are only aspects of greater Truths and that these in turn only form part of an ever expanding and more formidable perspective. Therefore, the Truth at any specific stage or time of an individual's development only consists of that degree of Divine expression that the aspirant can assimilate and interpret at his particular point of evolution.

"Raincloud of Knowable Things"

Man should constantly endeavour to keep his concept of the Truth vitally alive. Moreover, he should seek to replenish it from that inexhaustible reserve, symbolically known as the "Raincloud of Knowable Things" which the Hierarchy is providing on the higher mental and spiritual levels for the benefit of Humanity. Access to this "Raincloud" may be attained by men's aspiration to the 'good and true' by assiduous study and meditation and finally by loving understanding, goodwill and selfless service of fellow men.

Truth is a vibrant energy also manifested as Light, Love and Power, in other words, as Life itself. It finds expression in innumerable facets and variations, but as it never assumes a definite or final form, it is therefore not subject to clear definition. Because of this inherent vitality, Truth must always be granted full scope for growth and expansion. It should never be limited, allowed to become bound, crystallised or formalised and circumscribed by tradition or religious dogma. If thus confined or restricted, it will lose its character, becoming lifeless and therefore inanimate, colourless and ineffective – a mockery of Reality.

Truth Must be Freely Shared

To allow Truth full scope for development, it must never be selfishly retained for personal advantage, but should be freely shared with our fellow men. The joy of such sharing is one of the wonderful compensations of a life of redemption. When there is an aspiration and leaning towards Truth, it will also be realised that each individual will have his own interpretation and reaction to such Truth. Consequently, the aspirant should always be willing to offer and share his views freely, but care should be taken that these are never imposed on an unwilling or unsympathetic audience and neither should others be blamed for holding different points of view or sentiments.

It must also be remembered that with the passing on of any rendering of the Truth to its next point of destiny, something of its clarity or purity inevitably is sacrificed, particularly so when such concepts are intentionally reduced or adapted to provide a simpler version for or to accommodate the requirements of somewhat younger brothers on the Path of Life;

It would seem appropriate to conclude with the following words of an Elder Broth:

"Work to bring spirituality to materiality. Work ever to reveal the Life processes to Humanity. Work to expose the beauty of Divine Purpose to the mind of the human race. Work to inspire men to expansion and Truth, and work to redeem Humanity from the bondage of darkness into the freedom of Light. And as you work, the hand of a Brother will guide you; the Light will reveal the Truth to you; the Wisdom will impel you to understanding, and the Love will embrace you and inspire you. Walk the Path, my brother, through all the years and all the paces with clear-eyed purity of motive, conviction and resolve. I shall watch you though you know me not, and if you work for the redemption of your fellow men, you will evoke the aid of your Brothers, who likewise serve and love, and who brood over all Humanity."

PART II

Life is complex

I

Crises

The World in Flux

All creation is composed of and sustained by energy which exists in a perpetual state of cyclic and pulsating movement. No created form can ever remain static. Everything therefore exists in a condition of constant change and adaptation, from moment to moment assuming fresh proportions and phases, though such variations may not immediately be apparent to the limited powers of human perception.

This natural law is also applicable to human daily life. These cyclic adjustments lead man to ever alternating points of either low activity, often characterised by depression, or to periods of rising activity which may culminate in climaxing conditions and phases of realisation and exaltation. The level at which both these points of low or high performance may occur will depend on the general state of development of the individual, becoming ever more accentuated with higher spiritual attainment and therefore with increased sensitivity and consciousness.

Man is not only the product of energy, but also serves as an instrument or relatively small focal point for the interplay, transmutation and redirection of various energies and forces. This instrument is however far more complicated than is commonly realised and consists not only of the more apparent physical body, but also of the closely associated etheric, emotional and mental bodies. These bodies constitute what is known as the 'personality', which in turn is to a varying extent controlled by the soul or the spiritual aspect. The effect or crisis occasioned by these recurring waves of energy will not only depend on the potency of such energy; what will also prove to be of crucial importance is whether in the instrument concerned it is the physical, the emotional, the mental or the spiritual aspect which is predominant and will therefore largely determine the nature of the reaction that may be expected. These factors will also decide whether the resulting effects will be externally displayed or will be of an inner and therefore of a hidden or secret nature. It may thus happen that although to outer observers an individual's life may seem to be proceeding smoothly and on a relatively even keel, severe crises and unrevealed storms may in fact be raging within, resulting in revolutionary changes in activities or attitudes towards life.

Stepping Stones for Progress

Although there is a natural tendency for man to seek a life of relative peace and quiet, in most instances a too severely regimented and regulated existence will soon begin to pall, leading to an urge for greater variety and adventure, because the soul has incarnated into the physical world to gain experience and thereby to grow. Although periods of rest and serenity may at times be required for recuperation and restoration of a degree of balance after strenuous effort, it is the recurring points of crisis which provide life with its essence which serve as the stepping stones for progress. It should be remembered, however, that for the more spiritually developed person, it is not so much the physical or emotional crises that are needed, but rather those pinnacles of mental experiences and moments of soul awareness, preceding expansions of consciousness and an inflow of Love and Light, which eventually find expression in some form of service to fellow men.

Today, the whole of humanity is passing through a period of worldwide crisis. In many respects, it is of such an acute nature that many live in a perpetual state of fear, only recognising the immediately dangers and tensions. They thus fail to identify themselves with the sometimes partly hidden opportunities which are nonetheless increasingly available to everyone wishing to contribute their share towards an improved future for the human race. These times of crisis may therefore actually be turned to rich reward if faced with the necessary detachment and impersonality – provided activities are motivated with inner discernment and loving understanding, with tolerance for the points of view and activities of others and with the consecrated and unswerving objective of serving not only Humanity, but also the Hierarchy and the Divine Plan.

In the life of the individual, every point of crisis involuntarily leads to decision-making of some nature. These decisions develop into points of tension in which energy is accumulated, focussed where needed, culminating in mental perception and shaping into thoughts and ideas. This in turn is succeeded by a point of emergence when the ideas take on form and emerge into the field of practical activity and experience.

As a result of man's free will, the points of mental or spiritual crisis experienced are, however, not solely decided by outer circumstances or by the impact of energies lying beyond his command. No, to a large extent he can personally assume control of and become responsible for many of the crises influencing his path through life. In this connection it is well to keep in mind that a life which is devoid of crises becomes stagnant and therefore meaningless, valueless and a waste of time. By means of the free will, climaxing conditions can however be deliberately directed towards good or evil, solely depending on whether the individual is selfishly motivated or inspired by goodwill and altruism; in other words, depending on whether he is driven by the flesh or the spirit. It is therefore the intensity of purpose and will and the extent to which this is directed by the soul which will determine whether ruling circumstances, crises and tensions may be turned to good effect and applied to the advantage of the race and, as a secondary consideration, for personal progress.

There are however always outer obligations which have to be considered and met, but these must first be related to and suitably oriented towards inner requirements and responsibilities. Man is thus constantly faced with crises which afford him opportunities for reaching decisions which, for the time being or even the next cycle, will determine the direct of his Path and the tempo of progress. In this respect, it becomes crucial to be able to discriminate between the essential and non-essential, between those things which concern the temporary satisfaction of emotions and of the personality, but at the same time taking into account the inner needs of the soul.

The degree of progress attained by the spiritual aspirant is indicated by his success in handling the crises with which he is confronted. Every crisis may be regarded as a progressive field of opportunities and tests presented along his path of unfoldment. Every crisis successfully mastered will provide a new arena for extending his vision, for gaining knowledge and for attaining clearer insight and awareness thus enabling more effective use of the energy and light of the soul.

Mental and spiritual crises are periods of inner upheaval, strain and agitation, but with adroit handling, they may have far reaching consequences. Often these points of crisis are the harbingers of new revelation, fresh insight and clearer understanding of that which has been present but has remained obscure. When the state has been reached where the personality is in atunement with the soul, then during times of intense urgency, stress or trial, the compelling need will be communicated through the soul to spiritual sources. Thus, the necessary energy as well as the light and inspiration for its correct application will be provided, ensuring release, liberation and guidance for the individual along his path of spiritual unfoldment.

Notable Points of Crisis

The life of the human being is subject to several cycles of energy expression. Of these, the seven-year cycles probably play the most decisive role, being responsible for clearly discernible periods of crisis in many lives. This especially applies to those who have already entered the Path of Return and in whim, to lesser or greater extent, the soul is striving for dominance. According to the Tibetan, five notable points of crisis will typically occur during the life of each average but intelligent aspirant:

1. The state when the physical sheath is appropriated by the soul, which usually occurs between the ages of four and seven. Before this, the soul merely serves in an overshadowing capacity.
2. Between the fourteenth and eighteenth year, or during adolescence, the soul takes charge of the emotional body.
3. Between the twenty-first and twenty-fifth year the mental body is similarly appropriated and the man consequently begins to react to the soul's incentives.
4. Between the thirty-fifth and forty-second year further crises are experienced, which will lead to conscious contact with the soul.

5. The fifth crisis is manifested between the ages of fifty-six and sixty-three, which represents the point of culmination in the systematically increasing affinity between the soul and personality. This crisis determines the further effectiveness of this relationship and the extent to which it can be actively used as an instrument for serving humanity.

The first three of these crises will as a rule occur quite unconsciously, but this will not in the least detract from their importance in the unfolding life of the individual. Basic life changes will however often become apparent around the ages of thirty-five, forty-two, fifty-six and sixty-three. These adjustments may prove dramatic, sometimes entailing considerable adjustments and adaptations when, for instance, as a result of some unforeseen incident, new vistas have suddenly opened up to the mind's eye, resulting in the renouncing of firmly held concepts and their being supplanted with completely new ideas.

Although there are today many young people expressing considerable interest in spiritual matters, and that often at a relatively early age, mental maturity generally is not attained until the age of thirty-five.

Even though the aspirant may have been an active worker for many years, this time must as a rule be regarded as largely of a formative nature. It is only after reaching the above-mentioned age of crisis that his life-plan will become more clearly defined and will assumed more definite direction. Major adjustments will naturally have to be expected in subsequent years, but the probability is that such changes will also be patterned on these seven-year cycles.

The age of sixty-three often proves of special significance in the life of disciples. It is characterised by culminating tensions accrued as a result of the activities of preceding years, which at this stage reach a point of climax. It is of paramount importance that the disciple be able to recognise this vital stage with its supreme inherent opportunities, as this crucial phase may proffer optimal conditions for determining the nature of his terminal period of service during the present life-span.

Crises may either be of an objective or subjective nature. When they function on the physical plane, they may prove pleasant or painful, to a greater or lesser degree. However, with regard to their long term effect on the life of the individual, they will be of far less significance than those crises effecting the spiritual life. Spiritual crises, which frequently remain unrecognised, arise as the result of rhythmic pulsations in the world of matter and it is by applying the needed spiritual rhythms that man can surmount them and benefit from the tendered opportunities. Man should therefore learn not to avoid crises, notwithstanding the temporary hardships they might entail. It should be realised that life in fact consists of nothing but a succession of smaller or greater crises. In the final analysis, these emergencies merely represent points of scrutiny for the observance of the objectives of the soul and for determining the corresponding purity of motive and success achieved by the personality. When the imposed barriers have been surmounted, they will give rise to increased confidence and expanded vision, providing the courage, knowledge and eventually wisdom, to advance on to new fields of exploration on the ever extending Path, thereby enriching not only the life of the individual, but contributing towards the creation of a better world for mankind.

It is not only the individual whose life is subject to these periodic crises. As a matter of fact, the human race as a whole is presently being subjected to a blended range of energies of exceptional potency having a unique effect on the history of human affairs. Humanity is experiencing a period of spiritual crisis which is serving as a clearing process characterised by the breaking down, scrapping and discarding of many of the older, crystallised political, economic, social and religious systems which, though serving their purpose in the past, have since become obsolete. These are now being supplanted with fresh concepts. In many respects, this process is painful and because man as a rule lacks clear vision, it oftentimes happens that that which is outworn is destroyed before a suitable replacement is ready. This is characterised by temporary maladjustments and even chaos. However, step by step the needed adaptations will be effected, introducing the New Age which man is now hesitantly entering, opening up new vistas and opportunities for those with the necessary vision and motivated by the urge to serve.

Crises in History

In the past, history of Humanity has been qualified at various times by periodic appearances of divine envoys or prophets. Such advents have invariably been preceded by racial crises and rampant evil, inducing the masses to invocative appeal for Divine help. Notwithstanding man's material and mental achievements during the past centuries, mankind has today reached a similar stage of serious spiritual crisis. Christ's prescriptions of two thousand years ago, calling for mutual love and goodwill, have largely been disregarded, negated or misinterpreted and in many cases have been superseded by hate, selfishness and separativeness. All this has led to appalling conditions of human relationships and to a renewed supplication by the masses throughout the world for divine relief, inevitably setting the stage for the early reappearance of the Christ. This time, He may guide Humanity as a whole into a state of consciousness which will give birth to a civilisation where improved human relations, co-operation, understanding, goodwill and synthesis will form the universal keynote.

In conclusion, it is crucial that it be kept in mind that Humanity is now passing through a period of unusual crisis, stimulation and opportunity. What makes this crisis assume even greater importance, is that it happens to coincide with a parallel hierarchical crisis in which the Hierarchy and Humanity are jointly and independently striving towards the same purpose. Humanity is weary of the injustices and inequities of life, of constant war and fighting, of power politics and racial discriminations, of people perishing of want, hunger and misery. The masses are craving and aspiring for peace, for a fair and reasonable distribution of life's necessities and Nature's gifts and pining for sound human relations, goodwill and mutual understanding. This approach to life presently apparent through the world, is largely the result of hierarchical inspiration. Furthermore, it is the urgent objective of the Hierarchy that human problems be adjusted and resolved by the introduction and acceptance of these timeless values and that Humanity and the world at large be guided and ruled by the Laws of Spirit. These combined efforts will inevitably succeed and, within the relatively near future, will culminate with the coming of the Christ!

II

Freedom

The Awakening Urge for Freedom

Few words are probably more tritely used these days than 'freedom'. It is being applied in many nuances of meaning, such as freedom of the individual, of groups, communities, nations or races; economic, political and religious freedom; freedom of the press, of speech, movement and action; freedom from want and freedom from fear and, finally, superseding all these and providing the crowning glory to freedom, there is spiritual freedom, implying liberation of the soul from the limiting shackles of the three worlds of human experience.

The awakening urge for freedom, which today is being evidenced at every level of human existence, must be regarded as a reflection of the increasing tendency towards spiritual awakening largely generated by the accentuated inflow of the Seventh Ray energies now inaugurating the New Age of Aquarius. These energies are making a considerable contribution towards emancipating the human soul from the bondage of phenomenal and astral domination. The nature of the various aspects of freedom sought for or achieved, are merely indicative of the progress made by the aspirant along the Path of Life leading through the deep waters of experience, sorrow, distress and sacrifice – until after the course of many incarnations the gates of deliverance are finally reached, when there will be no further need for return to this world of glamour, pain and tears.

For aeons and during the course of innumerable incarnations, man has remained cloistered in the world of phenomena and illusion, hardly being aware at all of the supernal worlds of Light and Love by which he is surrounded, and towards the more conscious discerning of which, he will consistently be led by destiny. However, once he has gained his first fleeting glimpse of the light of his own soul, has obtained an inkling of Reality, and has become aware of the glamour and darkness with which he has so far been enshrouded, then nothing will be able to withhold him from entering and treading the Path of Return, the Path that will lead him to spiritual freedom and to the welcoming arms of the Father, the All Spirit.

Opposing Forces

The attaining of the eventual destination of the Path is assured but whether this goal of release from the fetters of the worlds of glamour and illusion will be effected rapidly or slowly will solely depend on the degree of dedicated effort evinced by each individual. It is all a question of becoming aware of the dualities of the astral plane and of the interacting pairs of opposites. Primarily, the struggle will be for dominance of the soul over its vehicle, the personality, which in turn will signify the gaining of spiritual freedom from the encumbrances of matter. For such liberation it is essential that man should find the point of balance between the pairs of opposing forces. By thus balancing these forces within his own nature he not only discovers the Path, but also succeeds in assimilating himself with the Path, thereby becoming a worker and server, not in the first instance for personal and selfish purposes but to assist with the redemption of his fellow man and of humanity as a whole. By turning the desires of man's astral nature into aspiration, he eventually succeeds in freeing himself from the wheel of rebirth which has controlled him for ages, thus releasing himself from the necessity of further reincarnation.

In this struggle towards the Light, fellow workers should be helped where required, but care should always be exercised not unduly to impose one's own ideas and interpretations upon others. People should be left free to use their own devices and minds, because that which is right for one person and under the circumstances which determine his life, will not necessarily apply in the same way or similar degree to the next.

Free Will

Although man disposes of a free will and at all times has the freedom of choice for directing his decisions and line of action, it should nonetheless be realised that such freedom remains very much a relative concept. On entering the Path and on becoming aware of the light and guidance of the soul, the free will of the personality will inevitably be subjected and curtailed to the same degree that the soul has taken charge. By introducing the light of the soul, new prerogatives and responsibilities are automatically assumed and if these responsibilities at times prove irksome to the personality, they may perhaps be temporarily evaded or ignored, but in the long run the demands of the soul will have to be recognised and acceded to. In comparison to personality criteria the soul is perfectly free, but the soul is nonetheless inextricably bound by the Law of Service and only retains a free choice in deciding the nature of such service. The recalcitrant personality, insisting on its freedoms, can therefore temporarily retard progress, but eventually the soul will not be denied and its demands will have to be complied with.

The freedom of action of soul-infused disciples is furthermore not only restricted by the obligations of the individual soul, but also has to be co-ordinated with the responsibilities of the group with which the particular soul is intimately linked. Actually it will be found that the disciplines of group-life may even be more demanding on personality freedom than self-imposed controls.

Freedom is a State of Mind

Freedom must therefore be realised as being largely a state of mind rather than representing freedom of action and that is where so many are inclined to misplace the accent, unduly emphasising physical freedom rather than availing themselves of their unalienable freedom of mind – thereby gradually recognising the inexhaustible and far greater opportunities offered by the worlds of subtler being and spiritual freedom.

In this life of service the disciple must learn the art of freeing himself and obtaining inner detachment from the clinging hands and clamouring demands of those with whom he is associated or whom he is trying to assist in their painful struggle to find their way along the Path of Life. Only by learning to stand detached and unafraid in the inner stronghold of the soul, will the server be enabled to work with true discrimination and loving understanding in his endeavours to meet the needs of those by whom he is surrounded.

On the other hand the disciple will find that he can never be really free, because he is never treading the Way alone and is always in the company of fellow travellers, whose interests must at all times be considered. For this purpose, Rules of the Road have been provided which must be mastered and obeyed in conjunction with individual laws, which in many instances will have to be superseded or adapted to group laws. He may therefore glory in his emancipation from the emotional or mental control of teachers or from those who stood in authority during his phenomenal life, but at the same time he should guard against being trapped by the 'glamour of freedom' which can so readily obscure his vision and restrict his effective service and progress, and which will always be subject to the more comprehensive rules governing group recognition, group efforts and group service. He will therefore have to learn to recognise his true associates with whom he has to travel and collaborate upon the Path, to adapt his service activities to theirs and to obey the higher rhythms and laws controlling group life, consciousness and service. This regime will ultimately also provide the avenue of admittance to the 'silent world' where the Masters of Wisdom will be found and where the worker will in turn be subjected to the laws of the spiritual realms, leading finally to inclusion in some Master's group and sphere of activity.

Therefore, although human progress consistently leads to greater freedom from personality control as well as from control by other personalities and conditions ruling in the three worlds of men, such freedom is only achieved because of a reciprocating and superseding control, at first by the clear and unimpeded light of the soul and subsequently by the Spirit. Furthermore, there can never be any escape or freedom from the Laws of Service or from the interaction between men, whether commanded by individual or group interests or whether applicable on personality or soul levels.

Religious or Church Domination

All established world religions are today being faced with the problem that the average man is coming into revolt against the spiritual domination exercised by the churches. In the minds of men there is a dawning recognition of freedom, which in their religion is brought to expression as a determination to assert their spiritual inclinations and aspirations in their own way. They want to be liberated from ancient expressions of religion which have become crystallised, with the emphasis so often still upon outer display, rituals and ceremony, in many instances distinguished by pomp and authority and supported by the power of money and possessions. Man is reaching the stage where he is insisting on freedom of thought and wants to unfold his own concepts and arrive at his own conclusions with regard to the Truth, no longer wishing to remain limited by ancient doctrines and dogma formulated centuries ago for people living under totally different circumstances and conditions. Many churches apparently do not yet realise that Truth is a viable energy in a constant process of growth, unfoldment and adaptation to changing circumstances. Consequently, there can never be finality in its presentation. The interpretation, formulation and proclaiming of Truth should therefore keep pace with the times, conforming to both the spiritual and mental evolution of successive generations.

Insistence on greater freedom with regard to religious thought is certainly no indication of a reduced sense of divinity, but to the contrary, is indicative of a rapidly growing awareness of inner realities. Man is no longer satisfied with formal outer demonstrations of religious practice. He wants to understand, contact and live up to those deeper spiritual verities to which he is awakening. Furthermore, he is increasingly becoming aware of the duality of existence, of the freedom of his soul, of its individual and group relations to the worlds of spirit and, even more particularly, that this soul cannot be subjected to the authority of dogmatic dictates of religious institutions or churches.

The key note of the modern world is freedom – freedom from want, freedom to live, to think, to know and to plan. The release of Humanity from the burdens of political suppression and religious and economic restrictions will come with man's progressive entry into the New Age. Many are as yet totally unaware of this process which is now in active course of realisation and of which the present day social unrest is only symptomatic. These rapid changes in all associated spheres of human living and activity throughout the world, which are upsetting so many of the firmly established customs and conditions and are breaking down all that has been achieved by man's selfish striving and ideological objectives of the past, should be seen as part of the preparatory stage for the manifestation of the New Regime for which man is now being equipped.

Yes, this liberation from the trammels of the past – the products of human selfishness and desire – will in many respects prove to be a painful business and will only be accomplished step by step with the persistent application of the energy of Love, with which Humanity is now systematically being irradiated from supernal spheres. The effects of this radiation are now being evinced as a gradual but nonetheless consistently growing spiritual awakening, evidenced by greater tolerance, understanding and an increasing awareness of the brotherhood of man, which will eventually result in a greater synthesis of Humanity as a whole, a general release from the thraldom of fear, a deepening realisation of the freedom of the soul and of the role it fulfils in the many spheres of human activity. This transition will simultaneously be characterised by the systematic improvement of human relationships.

Liberation of the human spirit will therefore be denoted by the emancipation of the soul from the shackles of the past and from the hold of the phenomenal worlds of emotion and desire, thus achieving freedom to move forward to new spheres of spiritual activity.

Liberation and Initiation

The Path of Liberation is esoterically also known as the Path of Initiation. To a large extent initiation may thus be regarded as a graded series of liberations from the emotional and mental aspects which in the past confined the soul to the three worlds from which it is now seeking release. This means attaining that freedom which will allow the soul the needed scope for its final unfoldment and absorption within the Monad.

Viewed from this approach, the various initiations may be regarded as depicting the following freedoms:

First initiation: Gaining freedom from the desires of the physical nature, indicating Birth into the Spiritual Kingdom.

Second initiation: Gaining freedom from and control over the emotional nature: the phase of the Baptism.

Third initiation: Gaining freedom from the control of the threefold personality or the phase of Transfiguration.

Fourth initiation: Gaining freedom from self-interest, therefore renouncing all forms of personal concern and concentrating the attention on the weal of Humanity as a whole: the stage of Renunciation.

Fifth initiation: Gaining freedom from the limitations of all aspects of vision, thus leading to Revelation.

There are similarly also 'freedoms' which concern each of the higher initiations, but these will not be dealt with here as they are commanded by concepts beyond ordinary human understanding.

The basic purpose of the Forces of Light is the liberation of Humanity from the limitations of the three worlds, but their work remains restricted by the fact that man must be allowed free choice and decision to achieve this goal of freedom. Should such freedom be bestowed on man without personal exertion of all the powers at his disposal, it would prove to be meaningless, because only that which man has earned by persistent strain and effort will ever prove to be of lasting value.

Conclusion

To conclude, it can be stated categorically that all human suffering derives from man's inborn selfishness and desire and it is only by relinquishing this selfish desire and by superseding it with love, sacrifice and service of the fellow man that liberation from the shackles of the three worlds will be gained.

Over whatever freedoms man may dispose, it should always be remembered that, just as is the case with any other principle or energy, freedom may also be abused and turned to adverse purposes. This negative aspect is for instance commonly demonstrated by mankind's indiscriminate use of the freedom of speech, causing so much injury and misery in this world of ours. What is even far worse, however, is that these wrongs are not always the result of lack of discernment or judgement, but that harm or mischief is all too often inflicted with deliberate and even cruel intent. Freedom is also often abused by using it for satisfying purely selfish desires and personal objectives to the detriment or total disregard of group or communal interests.

Notwithstanding all that has been written above about this vaunted freedom of the human being, a sober and dispassionate contemplation of all available evidence can only lead to the final conclusion that freedom, at whatever state of development, remains a most relative, elusive and often largely illusionary concept, constantly remaining subject to change, because at each different level of unfoldment of the human consciousness new facets of being are revealed and brought to recognition by the ever expanding inner vision. Man may therefore be released from the control of the more primitive emotional and desire life, but only to be restricted anew by a growing awareness not only of his dependence on, but also of his responsibilities towards his fellow man. Although his soul may experience a greater sense of freedom, that soul will never be able to escape the bonds of being an intrinsic part and remaining in close association with the brotherhood of Humanity, which in turn again forms part of the Greater Whole, the ONE!

III

The Equality of Man

The Human Kingdom of Nature

According to esoteric concepts, all human being belong to the Human Kingdom of nature, which represents the intermediate or transitional phase between the Animal and Spiritual Kingdoms. Considered as such, all men are classified under a single natural category, the members of which are spread in differing densities, diverse qualities and varying circumstances over all the continents of the world.

All natural kingdoms or everything constituting creation, exist in a ceaseless state of change and evolution. The whole of each Kingdom is thus composed of individual specimens at every possible phase of evolution. The complete potential range includes those still at the lowest levels of development and culminating with those who over the aeons have passed through every phase of experience and modification for which the evolutionary plan provides. As far as man is concerned, the latter stage means reaching the top rung of the ladder and preparing for transition to the Spiritual Kingdom.

The many races, nations, communities or groups composing mankind are widely divergent as to colour, physique, culture, civilisation, language, creed and intelligence. Nonetheless, in totality they form the One Humanity, essentially governed by the same fundamental nature, all being derived from a common source, all subject to the same natural laws and all evolving towards the same mental and spiritual objectives. It is these basic and divine attributes which serve as a common bond of equality between men, eventually providing each individual with an equal opportunity for progressive unfoldment and ultimate attainment.

Men belong to the same genus, all forming part of the One Humanity, within which every single composing member constitutes a separate unity. Although each of these units may in many respects resemble or conform with other associates, groups or races, each nevertheless, retains his own specific combination of characteristics which distinguish him from every other individual specimen, thus identifying him as a unique being.

The Inherent Nature of Man

But before the equality of man can be considered with discrimination, there has to be a clear understanding of the inherent nature of man and of the aspects on which comparisons are to be based. Of primary consideration is the duality of man, referring to the fact that he is constituted of what is known as the 'Personality' or the material aspect, which merely serves as the vehicle for expressing the second or spiritual aspect, the immanent Soul.

Each individual soul represents a small fraction or component of the Divine Spirit, the One Soul. It is this relationship which provides the magnetism synthesising all souls and therefore all men into the One Humanity. However, immediately the question arises: if there exists this common bond, then why is it that so little is noticed of this vaunted unity and brotherhood amongst men and why this perpetual perverseness, hate, enmity and separateness so typical of man's daily relationships?

The problem lies in the fact that although each infant body is provided with an incarnating soul at the time of birth, this soul remains in a relatively dormant condition in the average person. It only begins to asset itself when that particular soul reaches a fairly advanced state in its evolutionary development, which stretches over aeons and innumerable reincarnations. Therefore in the early stages of development it is not the soul that governs man's attitude and qualities, but the 'Personality', which in turn is a triplicity composed of the body of flesh, the emotional or astral body and the mental body. The nature, tendency or disposition of the individual will largely depend on which of these bodies is in the ascendancy.

Disparities in Man

The vast majority of mankind are still at the stage where they are controlled by their emotions. Fortunately, there are increasing numbers who are beginning to be mentally oriented and who are consequently also coming progressively under soul direction. These widely varying stages in development are often responsible for the striking differences in 'equality' between various individuals, groups, nations and races. The divergent attributes are largely emotionally founded and directed by selfish desire in its main facets of expression. Only when the soul is gradually gaining dominance are its outstanding quality of Light and Love slowly brought to the fore and granted the opportunity of clearer definition.

The following are the principal factors giving rise to these racial, regional or individual disparities:

1. Man's karmic background or, in other words, the effects of activities not only of the immediate past, but often of happenings dating far back to distant historic times. It is a natural law that every action is inevitably followed by a commensurate reaction. Consequently, present day circumstances and the appearance, quality and characteristics of mankind as a whole or of its many composing elements, are often directly or indirectly due to incidents or activities of the past. Similarly, this Law of Cause and Effect will, to a large extent affect the future, not only of nations, but also the time, place and circumstances of reincarnation of individual souls.

2. The vibrant quality, magnetism and colouring of individuals is essentially affected by the basic combination of cosmic Rays of Energy to which every form of life is consistently subject.

3. Closely associated with the Ray effects are the astrological influences. The energies radiated from various celestial bodies undoubtedly play a considerable role, but the correct human interpretation of their effect often remains questionable. Astrological forces primarily effect the consciousness or soul aspects and the extent of these reactions therefore largely depends on the point of evolution already attained, exhibiting a proportionate decrease in accordance with the degree of control exercised by the soul over the personality.

4. Each human race is distinguished by its own particular differences in colour of skin, of form, speech and character, thus endowing each individual member of a race with certain specific and inherent racial qualities, characteristics or thought-forms.

5. As already indicated, each individual will furthermore be differentiated by the evolutionary status achieved and whether the life intent is focussed in the physical, emotional, mental or spiritual aspects.

The Right to Freedom

Today there is a growing realisation throughout the world of the relative and inherent right to freedom of every human being. However, an essential part and condition of such freedom is that the individual shall exhibit that responsibility of action and attitude towards his fellow man, community or nation which is expected or demanded of him. He should conform to not only the proclaimed and recognised civil laws of the community, but also to the unwritten laws of common decency, consideration, understanding, patience, unselfishness and goodwill towards those with whom he is associated and where the vagaries of destiny have placed him for some specific purpose.

In practice it will be found that the correct use or conversely, the abuse made of personal freedom, will largely depend on the evolutionary stage attained by the individual or group concerned. This again boils down to the fact that although all men belong to the one human brotherhood and are endowed with the same ultimate spiritual potential, their unfoldment takes place over aeons of time and is the cumulative result of experience gained during the course of innumerable reincarnations. The consequence is that in terms of physical expression, the human lives represented on Earth at any one time will cover a very wide range in disparity whether viewed from the points of physical, emotional, mental or spiritual development.

Although every form of autocratic action or rule should be questioned and avoided, the principles and effectiveness of democracy as applied today are often overrated and based on illusion. In fact, the decisions to which the masses react are not the product of their own thinking, but merely the outcome of ideas with which they have been infused and which originate from leaders or members of the intelligentsia, who generally propagate these thoughts and schemes for some specific personal purpose. Unfortunately, the masses still readily lend themselves to instigation by agitators. There are for instance those who are led to strive or even fight for such principles as "the equality of man" or for "one man, one vote", without any real concept of the implications of underlying principles and with the capacity to discriminate clearly or analyse these matters for themselves. Consequently, their reactions are largely formulated, stimulated and manipulated by opportunities. The man in the street who reflects what is known as "public opinion" is still primarily focussed on the emotional level. This means that his thinking remains limited to the lower mind which mainly concerns his physical needs and emotional life. As a rule, the general public is as clay in the hands of the adroit manipulator well versed in mass-psychology, who by oratory or writing knows how to direct and sway the emotions of the multitudes. Although this aptitude for guiding public opinion in a specific direction has been badly abused in the past by crafty and often unscrupulous political agitators, who manage to twist or reduce idealistic principles to a pathetic farce, these same attributes can also be turned to common advantage. During the New Age, they will be used effectively by inspired and altruistic leaders to steer humanity into clearer light and a better future.

Man is now, however, entering the stage where the numbers of those who are following the mental approach to life are rapidly increasing. This advance is attended by a simultaneous growth in the number of those in whom the soul is showing a tendency towards taking a stronger command over the personality. Consequently, there exists an accentuated expression of the spiritual nature and therefore of the duality of man.

In the coming New Age there will no longer be the question of class domination; of an aristocracy which over the ages has entrenched itself and ruled the lives of the proletariat, mainly for personal gain and self-glorification; nor will there be the domination by a strong capitalistic system over the labour forces, which often results in ruthless exploitation. On the other hand, it is often found, today, that the pendulum has swung back to the other extreme, where the workers have come into revolt and have gained the upper hand by availing themselves of their numeric strength and the fact of their forming an essential part of the production machine. Unfortunately, in their lust for revenge and craving for power, they are abusing and thereby undermining their new-found position and acquired advantages by often blindly striking out not only at the evils of the capitalistic system, but thus also destroying many basically sound structures of both communal living and the means of production.

What is needed is leadership based on altruism, personal and group integrity, intelligence, vision, experience and understanding of life, striving to achieve the greatest benefit for the large number or, in other words, to work for the common good. The basis should therefore be discriminative goodwill, tolerance and loving understanding, allowing each individual the maximum freedom compatible with communal requirements and offering opportunity to each and everyone for maximum development of inherent potentials. This should lead to a spirit of active responsibility, ruled by an attitude of "all for one and one for all".

True Brotherhood Among Men

Real equality in daily living has never existed and will never be achieved. The nearest approximation of 'equality' can only be attained by a thorough understanding of the principles responsible for the wide disparity existing in the several attributes by which man is qualified. This should then lead to a proper sense of proportion, self-understanding and an appreciation of man's relation to others and the world as a whole. The first prerequisite for such realisation is a clear awareness of the effective functioning, firstly of the natural Law of Rebirth and, secondly, of the closely associated Law of Cause and Effect. Such understanding can only emphasise the absurdity of using the favourite assertion that "all men are equal" when referring to man in the narrower sense of daily existence.

True brotherhood among men is something that will eventually be realised. However, it is a principle and life-theme that will only be developed gradually, because it is founded on an inner evolutionary approach to life and is not a matter that can be imposed on man by any form of compulsion.

That differences in stages of development should be recognised and acknowledged, is therefore only proper and the logical conclusion to an objective consideration of life's circumstances. Nevertheless, special care should be taken that such recognition does not lead to any semblance of a spirit of superiority and separateness, which inevitably leads to the creation of barriers and tension between men or, on a higher level, between nations and races. All men belong to the One Humanity and need each other, as different types and characters are essential and complementary for integrating, synthesising and fulfilling the divine Purpose. Whatever his qualities, no man can ever stand absolutely alone if he intends to progress and to achieve the objectives for which his soul was brought into incarnation. Therefore, to make a success of life there should always be mutual understanding, tolerance, goodwill and helpfulness to satisfy that inner need, so often unrealised, for mutual companionship and intercourse.

In conclusion, it may be said that although all men are potentially equal, referring both to their origin and destiny, in terms of practical existence, men are far from equal. They differ in every possible respect, encompassing the complete scope of physical, emotional and mental development, expressing every conceivable combination of the infinite characteristics encountered in these several spheres of living.
Mankind therefore includes:
- those who are still bestial, in comparison with those who are nearing the angelic stage;
- the crude and the refined;
- the emotional, the mental and the spiritual types;
- those living solely for satisfying their selfish physical urges and appetites, as compared with those who hardly consider their own bodily needs, concentrating their attention on the subjective worlds and on attempts at serving their fellow men.

In daily life these differences are so marked and obvious that, for present purposes, a more detailed analysis will prove futile. The important point to be stressed, however, is that these inequalities should not be the cause for separateness. Rather should they prove an added incentive for those already fairly advanced along the evolutionary Path, to forget their personal progress or assumed superiority, allowing them to turn back to lend a helping hand to those still struggling along in the relative darkness of lower levels. Thereby will they not only promote the upliftment of less favoured brothers, but will simultaneously contribute towards synthesising and achieving the ultimate objective of uniting all men into the One Humanity!

IV

SHARING THE GIFTS OF LIFE

The Bounties of Life

It is only as the mind of man progressively unfolds that he increasingly becomes aware of, appreciates and becomes more closely identified with the multiplicity, diversity and astounding richness of the bounties of Life endowed him by the Supreme Being on his Path of Experience. Owing to man's lack of understanding, many aspects of nature at first appear to be unbalanced, resulting in various forms of conflicting interests, competition and innumerable phases of struggle for existence. During this process each individual, impelled by selfish desire and greed, tries to secure the maximum share to which he considers himself entitled, of that which life has to offer. But apart from such self-justification, if the opportunity presents itself, many will not hesitate for a moment to appropriate that which he realises rightly belongs to or is due to others.

As man evolves his demands grow beyond his initial physical and emotional desires to include urges for gratifying certain mental requirements which, in turn, are eventually superseded by spiritual aspirations. While man still functions on the lower levels of existence, his nature remains basically selfish, which to a certain extent is understandable, as at that stage, life is still a continuous struggle for survival and self-protection. This is accompanied by an inherent urge for self-improvement expressed as self-assertion and greed, and reflected as a striving for possessions, riches, social status and power.

It is only after every possible phase of physical, emotional and mental life has been gratified during the course of aeons and innumerable lives, that man slowly begins to realise the dual nature of existence and gradually becomes aware of the presence of the Self – the Soul. He then comes to the realisation of the futility and emptiness of striving to satisfy merely the physical and emotional desires and ambitions, for there is so much more for which to aspire – the beauty and reality of the spiritual spheres! Step by step the aspirant's outlook on life is being changed; he comes to realise the relative insignificance of human existence on Earth in relation to the position man occupies in the Solar System and even more so when compared to the greater Universe! He becomes vaguely aware of higher spheres of existence, of the presence of a vast but only faintly conceivable organisation of divine and cosmic Entities, under the direction of a Supreme Being, entrusted with the execution of an as yet totally incomprehensible divine Purpose and Plan! He begins to perceive that this exalted organisation is reflected on our puny little planet Earth by our own Deity or Lord of the World, supported by an extensive and graded Hierarchy of Spiritual Beings. Finally, he comes to the realisation that he forms a small but integral part of Humanity, which in turn only represents one of the seven Kingdoms of Nature comprising our earthly existence. As such and as a self-conscious unit of this Human Kingdom, there are certain responsibilities he must fulfil to comply with the demands of the hierarchical Plan.

When man reaches this stage, the selfishness which for aeons has characterised his approach to life is slowly superseded by a radically changing attitude of altruism, by a deepening understanding of the purpose of Life and the incentives motivating the lives of his fellow human beings and an urge to identify himself with the higher demands of this spiritual world. Finally, he feels the need to share everything at his disposal, whether physical, emotional, mental and spiritual with his fellow men in an attempt to help uplift those who so far have lagged behind in man's joint struggle towards the Light.

The average human being takes it for granted that whether rich or poor, high or low on the social ladder, he has as much right as the next man to breathe the air of the common atmosphere. (Fortunately, as a rule he remains blissfully ignorant of the extent to which this air has already been polluted by human activity!) Similarly, he regards it as a matter of course that the majority of people are allowed to partake freely of the sunlight and rain with which nature in its many vagaries is providing the Earth. So often, however, people remain unaware of the fact of there being a multitude of more bounteous gifts that nature has in store for man and to which he is fully entitled, but of which, during the course of the ages, he has systematically been deprived by selfishness, greed, traditional customs and activities of either individuals, groups or nations. Just as man is allowed free access to the light and air of the heavens, so in the beginning he also had complete freedom of movement and could tread at will any part of the Earth lying within his reach, making free use of all its material aspects, whether of mineral, vegetable or animal nature. Gradually all this has been radically changed by human intervention, resulting in innumerable restrictions on the use, application and distribution of many of the gifts of Nature. That the increasing human population should have led to regulated and organised systems of living to ensure the fair allocation and distribution of the world's products and amenities would only be reasonable and welcomed by the vast majority. But this is not what happened, though it may constitute a minor aspect of the overall picture. What actually occurred is that over the ages, with the progress of so-called civilisation, the strong or mentally better equipped have systematically abused the privileges by which they were enabled to raise themselves above the masses. These favoured individuals have as a rule taken advantage of their somewhat superior mental gifts and proffered opportunities to grab and retain as much of the world's products as their covetous and grasping hands could lay hold of, thus enriching themselves at the cost of the less privileged. The consquence has been that for many centuries a minute percentage of humanity has been wallowing in luxury, while the majority have existed in relative poverty and squalor, often in abject misery, with hardly enough to feed, clothe and shelter themselves or their dependents. And thus even today there are still thousands dying annually of starvation and exposure.

These radical extremes in living conditions have at times driven the suppressed, exploited and impoverished masses to revolt, occasionally resulting in a temporary improvement on limited terrains, though more often leading to chaos and deteriorated conditions. Certainly, these uprisings have not succeeded in providing a satisfactory solution of the fundamental problems.

Gradually the proletariat has come to the realisation that the only means for effectively asserting themselves and exacting concessions from those in power and responsible for their exploitation, is by availing themselves of their numerical strength by presenting a united front by properly organising and co-ordinating their combined forces. During the present century this has led to a world-wide, open confrontation between what is termed Labour and Capital and to the emergence of various ideologies, of which communism has assumed a significant role.

All these collisions between the interests of man and man, group and group, nation and nation, resulting in rancour and bitter hatred, endless fighting, bloodshed, destructive and wasteful wars, arise from common sources which may be briefly outlined as:

(a) The inherent selfishness of man, evidenced by his greed, covetousness and attempts to grasp and hoard all that comes within his reach, whether needed or not, without any consideration for his neighbour, often begrudging him even the wherewithal for a bare existence.

(b) An urge for power, self-glorification and for dominating the fellow man.

(c) The inadequate and hopelessly disproportionate distribution and sharing of the riches and products of Nature.

(d) The existing inequality in the physical, emotional, mental and spiritual development of man, with the result that individuals are encountered at every level of unfoldment, with the majority functioning in the emotional stage, where their activities are still largely governed by their emotions and desires. A much smaller percentage are mentally controlled and guided by reason, leaving only a relatively limited number of individuals whose personalities have been completely superseded by their souls, thus allowing all their activities to be directed from spiritual levels.

(e) Another crucial factor accentuating the inequality of man is the fact that each individual or nation is being influenced by varying combinations of cosmic Energy Rays, resulting in distinctive but divergent reactions in the characteristics and accomplishments of those concerned.

(f) Finally, it can be stated that the above factors are mainly responsible for the hatred, intolerance, jealousy, criticism and suspicion which today are systematically sowing discord between men. It is only when such attitudes are superseded by Love, Tolerance and Understand, in other words, by the attributes of the Soul, that human relationships will truly begin to improve, leading to the more equitable sharing of life's profuse amenities.

Though the principles of sharing have been considered in general, it is felt that certain specific aspects deserve closer examination. This may perhaps entail a measure of repetition, but this is done deliberately to focus the attention and therefore accentuate certain features which are so often too readily overlooked.

The Art of Giving and Sharing

The dawning New Age, which man is now entering with hesitant steps, will largely be characterised by improved human relationships based on such attributes as goodwill and loving understanding. These qualities will gradually tend to arouse a greater spirit of coherence amongst individuals, an awareness of inner brotherhood and a spontaneous urge to share all that makes life worth living with the fellow man. This impulse to share is again but another expression of a growing need for closer collaboration with others, for group work and synthesis.

Apparently it takes many lives before man finally comes to the realisation that selfish grasping, and anxious and greedy retaining of that which has been acquired, brings no real or lasting happiness. No, the real joy of life is only attained by learning the art of giving and gladly sharing not only material possession, but also the emotional, mental and spiritual aspects. Man should always remember that inner pain is relieved when the relative problems are shared with others. Similarly, when friends are also allowed to share in one's joys, these joys are multiplied in accordance with the degree of sharing. It will therefore be found that, symbolically speaking, the richest men on Earth are actually those who have shed every form of selfishness, who are attaining inner completeness by freely sharing all that life has bequeathed. As with time and experience greater wisdom is achieved, man loses interest in his separated self and begins to realise more subtly and acutely that he forms an intimate part of the greater human community. Furthermore, he realises that to achieve his own spiritual progress and contentment, he must first forget about his personal interests and see that his neighbour profits in like or even greater measure, sharing every aspect of the advantages or progress accruing to him. It is this same trend of spirit which, today, on a broader level, is manifested in communities and nations as goodwill and welfare movements, clubs, fraternities, co-operatives and organisations such as the Red Cross, which work for the benefit of all mankind. Therefore, the recognition of the need for giving and sharing is step by step beginning to infuse the racial consciousness.

Those who have to yet learned to give freely, will also find that they lack free access to supply, as the Law of Substance is of a reciprocal nature. To evoke the stores of the spirit effectively the channel must first be prepared for its unrestricted distribution.

One of the most sublime gifts bestowed on man is to be favoured with a pure and unselfish spirit, imbued with a yearning to give and share. This grace can only be induced by a pure and loving soul. All those who have become aware of the Path of Light have automatically opened the flood-gates to the supplies of the subjective realms. This in turn is reflected in the achievements of a loving heart, by compassion and deep understanding and by liberally sharing the wisdom with which a life of experience, study and service has enriched the mind.

There is an esoteric law to the effect that "to those who give all, all is given". In practice numerous workers are inclined to limit themselves by withholding, and an unrealistic fear of releasing and liberating themselves by relinquishing all selfish attachments still binding them to that which is only of transient value. They forget that the doors to greater treasures can only be unlocked by unrestricted, heart-inspired and spontaneous giving. Once the worker is correctly attuned by following the dictates of the soul, he will find there to be no greater joy than giving and sharing his all with his fellow men!

Discriminative Sharing

The precepts set out above to the effect that man should share all he has with his fellow man are quite correct, but such sharing should nonetheless be judiciously performed and must not be purely emotionally inspired. That which is shared, whether material or subjective, is a form of energy and, like all energy, it can be applied either positively, effectively or even negatively. Therefore by sharing that which is available without discrimination, such offering may be either misdirected or misapplied, thus failing to fulfil its intended purpose. Even though such a bequest may have been rendered with the best intention and from a loving heart it might happen that the receiver is as yet unprepared, not having reached the stage where the proffered gift can be used effectively. In the latter instance, it might actually cause more harm than good, resulting in a total waste of energy which might have been applied with much greater consequence if correctly and discerningly distributed.

It should always be remembered that unless man has personally evoked that which is received by his attitude, endeavour, aspiration or action, thus deserving or earning such favours, these potential blessings will remain relatively meaningless to him and therefore largely unappreciated and wasted. It often happens that such unprepared persons or nations, after receiving undeserved gratitudes, loudly start claiming for more, regarding such benefits as their right. Meanwhile, they are not prepared to lift a finger or to make any effort towards earning their share of that which is so blatantly demanded, and which on receipt will probably be misapplied, dissipated or ineffectively squandered.

Nobody in this life should ever be allowed to die of hunger, exposure or any other form of want. At the same time, that which is provided over and above the marginal requirements of existence should figuratively be "earned in the sweat of one's brow". However, it stands to reason that this does not apply to the immature, the physically or mentally sick and unfit and to the aged and decrepit. Ample provision should be made to furnish these helpless ones with the needed loving care and maintenance. Furthermore, the opportunities and facilities should be provided for all those prepared to work, study or improve themselves in any direction for which they might show a special aptitude or inclination, thereby better qualifying them for productive work on behalf of their community.

The benefits accruing in life to any individual or group will eventually be commensurate not only with the effort or quantity of energy expended, but also with regard to its relative quality. The latter proviso refers specifically to the level at which the activity concerned takes place and whether it is mainly of a physical, emotional or mental nature. It will be found that as mental and spiritual characteristics evolve, a corresponding change in value will also take place. During the more elementary stages, the accent falls primarily on physical accomplishments and the sharing of advantages and pleasures of the more material aspects of existence. As man progressively advances along the evolutionary path, a noticeable change takes place, not only in the focus of his interests and activities, but also in his appraisal of those concerns, attractions and benefits which to him make life worth living. Certain material needs will definitely still have to be met to sustain the physical body, but the emphasis will now be increasingly directed towards satisfying the mental and spiritual requirements.

The problem is, however, that it takes a long time and man must be quite well advanced along the Path of Life before he is able to first recognise and subsequently to overcome the utter selfishness and greed inherent in all developing personalities. The normal tendency with man is to begin by abusing his growing intelligence, cleverness and skills by applying them purely for personal advantage. In practice it is found that these selfish procedures often prove to be detrimental to the interests of his less favoured and more retarded brothers. By greedily grasping and hoarding a disproportionate share of the Earth's products and that which has been gained by man's endeavours and ingenuity, those better favoured with intellect and by circumstances, but still in the grip of their selfishness, have discovered how to enrich themselves beyond all moderation at the cost of their fellow man.

This generally means unreasonable and superfluous benefits for the few, whilst millions have to exist below the bread line, many even perishing of want and misery. It is therefore quite understandable that the average man in the street is now revolting against these intolerable conditions of maladjustment and inequitable distribution of the products of the Earth. Furthermore, it should be remembered that one of the first prerequisites for entering the New Age is that these irrational disparities must be eliminated to a considerable extent.

All men are sons of God and therefore spiritual brothers, subconsciously or deliberately striving and moving towards a common objective. Meanwhile, a wide disparity exists with regard to the stage attained by various individuals along the Path of Life. As far as daily living is concerned, men are actually far from equal, with some already well ahead as they near human perfection, whilst the majority still lag behind, struggling in the dark, held back by the doldrums of physical and emotional existence. Perhaps these considerations might contribute something to expose the motives of many of those glibly advocating the "equality of man" and "one man, one vote". This theme is often used for deluding the unthinking and gaining their support to further specific political aims. In this connection, it should be generally understood that public policy and proceedings are not democratically formulated by the vote of the masses, but by the intellect and thoughts of relatively only few individual leaders, who chiefly are responsible for cleverly moulding and manipulating what is known as public opinion.

Because of this wide discrepancy in man's development and manifested aptitudes, there will be a corresponding difference in the quality and nature of the results yielded by his efforts. Consequently, it would be unrealistic to expect that men should share equally or be remunerated on the same basis for their widely varying contribution to the collective welfare. That a realistic distinction should exist between the benefits earned by different individuals is therefore not only fair and reasonable, but also inevitable. This disparity in the share as allocated to each individual should, however, be founded on a reasonable basis and should certainly not reach the extremes reflected under the present day social and economic systems.

Therefore, be willing and eager to share all that life provides so abundantly! However, at the same time, share with discrimination, carefully avoiding the dangerous pitfall of using injudicious discretion as an excuse for refraining from sharing generously and with loving understanding.

Money and Possessions

As man develops spiritually, he begins to realise that though the gathering of possessions and riches may be useful for promoting social status and prestige, for exercising greater authority and power over fellow men and for conveying a sense of satisfaction of relative achievement, such attainments nevertheless remain hollow emblems, bringing no real happiness. On the contrary, more often they lead to personal sorrow, frustration and distress when injudiciously and selfishly applied. When such abundance and power are abused, as happens only too frequently, widespread misery and hardship will be caused to all those associated with such transactions. Had the available energies been shared altruistically and used constructively, instead of with purely selfish intent, their effects would have been beneficial and in accord with their motivating cause.

When regarded subjectively, money is in fact nothing but materialised energy, an impersonal, blind force which can be used either negatively or positively, destructively or productively, altruistically or selfishly, either to the detriment or advantage of all concerned. Because its potentialities are so frequently misapplied, there are those who regard money as something unclean, forgetting that it can do great good if used for the right purposes with correct motivation. In the modern world, money has become an essential commodity, fulfilling a most useful function for the effective transfer of energy from one scheme, objective or activity to another, serving as an effective basis for our whole economic structure. It is therefore not the use of money as such that should be avoided. What actually should be subjected to careful examination are the underlying motives associated with its used. Whereas in the past money has often been the symbol of man's selfishness, it can and will at some future stage serve as an important instrument for implementing his goodwill.

The effective introduction and world-wide propagation of the principles on which the New Age are to be founded, will require considerable funds if the work is not to be unduly delayed. Such funds will inevitably be attracted and forthcoming if supported by altruistic motives and the proper techniques. In the first instance the symbolic value of money should be clearly realised in order that it may be regarded as a spiritual asset and correctly used on behalf of humanity. At present man's general attitude is to hold on tightly to his money and possessions in fear of the future and with distrust of his fellow men, of whom the majority, each on his own behalf, have been using every means at their disposal to grab and retain as large a portion as possible of Earth's products for their own selfish and personal purposes, without the least consideration for the interests of the next man, so often even showing no compunction whatsoever of depriving their neighbour of that which could be regarded as his fair and legitimate share. This most regrettable attitude must be changed as rapidly as possible. Furthermore, it should be realised that where individuals and groups are striving to administer money for the good and upliftment of their fellow men, there this need, when coupled with love and goodwill, will serve as a magnetic force which will unfailingly attract all the money genuinely required for the effective implementation of the work.

The past century or so has been characterised by a noticeable and growing sense of responsibility, perhaps attributable to a feeling of guilt on the part of many of the more opulent. In many instances such a guilty conscience is reflected as an urge to share the excess of surfeit possessions by channelling a smaller or larger part of the same through various welfare organisations to the poor and destitute. This certainly has been a trend in the right direction and must be regarded as indicative of a gradual spiritual awakening. But this kindling tendency is only the prelude to a totally new and far more comprehensive change in human relationships which will characterise the coming New Age. What is therefore urgently needed at this stage is a recognition of the spiritual nature of money and that apart from its material functions, it can also be dedicated towards divine purposes and therefore towards the realisation of the Divine Plan for out little planet. The spiritual unfoldment of humanity constitutes an essential part of this Plan.

The efforts of those who are endeavouring to reorientate money in general towards spiritual work by means of meditation, will be in vain if they do not first begin by redirecting the energies and money under their own control towards the visualised objective of serving mankind and thus the WHOLE. Vast funds are needed for the effective spreading of esoteric knowledge and principles, for organising the men of goodwill and promoting their activities and for preparing mankind for the reappearance of the Christ. Man should be made aware of the fact of the millions which today are being wasted not only ineffectively but harmfully on needless and futile luxuries, on various objects of inane desire, on an insatiable search for every possible form of excitement and diversion. Worst of all are the vast amounts being spent annually on armaments of every nature, either for the further enrichment of those financial magnates working unobtrusively from behind the scenes, or for the mutual destruction of nations. All this money should be deflected and redirected into constructive channels for promoting man's spiritual well-being and for overcoming his purely selfish and materialistic outlook of the past. By the wise use of the world's financial resources and by its discriminative sharing with those groups and institutions supporting a new and positive approach with regard to its application in the promotion of human well-being, the New Era will be introduced and the way opened for the selfless work of men of goodwill, thus leading to improved human relationships and preparing the way for the reappearance of Him for Whom all mankind is waiting!

Sharing World Resources

Nature has generously supplied the world with all the resources, energies and requirements needed by man for his well-being and to ensure his sustained evolutionary development. That apparent deficiencies occur is purely occasioned by the injudicious and selfish manipulation of existing resources and circumstances by the egotistical human element. With the course of time practically every form of natural resources occurring in a condition in which it can be unilaterally demarcated, claimed, reserved or withheld by self-seeking interests, whether individual, communal or national, has been and is being exploited by the few to the detriment of mankind in general. The result is that today, apart from the air we breathe and the light from the heavens, there remains very little that man can still freely acquire and use. For his daily needs man is largely dependent on the several moneyed interest or those in power, who are only willing to cede the produce of the Earth at a price on a discriminative and selective basis, leaving very little scope for genuine and fair sharing of the numerous and bounteous bequests of nature, the essentials of which should be available to every son of man.

It is this selfish and greedy attitude, so typical of human nature, that has been responsible for endless friction and strained human relationships, not only on personal levels, but also in national and international spheres. This provides the cause for endless disputes, fighting and bloody wars as each interested party in its rapacious greed either refuses to share equitably that over which it exercises controle or else is driven by an irresistible urge to acquire ever more assets, either for personal gratification or, as a rule, for achieving even greater power over fellow men.

A striking example of how the social and economic system of the whole world may be affected, unbalanced and disrupted by selfish, ill-advised, unbalanced control of natural resources which were destined by nature for humanity as a whole, is the way that the world's oil supplies have been exploited. At present the position has been reached where a few countries of which several, apart from their only recently acquired status as oil-producers, previously occupied relatively unimportant positions in the world economy – have suddenly emerged to the position where owing to their command of important sources of this strategic energy reserve, they can now literally dictate on prices to the world, even going so far as to abuse their hold over these essential energy resources for extorting international blackmail. What a pity that concerns or countries rendering themselves guilty of such public extortion do not realise that their practices must inevitably result in harmful repercussions and that apparent advantages acquired today by such unethical procedures must and will unavoidably end by bringing more harm than good to the countries and interests concerned.

As it is, if the Tibetan's prophecies are correctly interpreted, it seems doubtful whether humanity will much longer remain so utterly dependent on oil for its energy requirements. He intimates that novel techniques will be developed for the universal and inexpensive generation of electricity (energy) from either the atmosphere or water. These new systems will enable the production of energy at such minimal cost that it will literally be available to everyone for all purposes, thereby revolutionising standards of living. At the present stage, with the average individual's outlook and approach to life so adjusted to its material and commercial aspects and limitations, he can hardly form a clear picture of the fantastic changes which are apparently lying in store for him. Furthermore, it appears probable that these changes will not be relegated to some distant future, as man is now rapidly being prepared for their realisation and accomplishment. On the other hand, these visions can only be accorded and effectively implemented with corresponding changes in man's approach and relations to his fellow men. He must progressively learn to share with greater generosity and liberality those energies now at his disposal, and for which he is merely serving as a channel, so that those less favoured and still lagging behind can also be reached.

Therefore, man has to learn that when, owing to life's, circumstances, certain individuals, groups or nations happen to have been placed in positions in time and space where they have gained control over specific products of nature, these resources do not belong to them exclusively. Rather, these temporary controllers should be regarded as the trustees of supplies belonging to mankind as a whole. It is therefore their responsibility to see that these assets are developed and distributed on an equitable basis to all those individuals, communities or nations in need of the product.

Because of widely varying climatic and soil conditions in which water supplies so often prove to be the limiting factor, certain regions or countries are much better adapted for food production than others. These disparities in the basic potentials provided by nature are further accentuated by the fact that certain nations are scientifically and technically far more advanced and proficient than others. Consequently, they make more effective use of existing conditions, often producing specific food crops in considerable excess of local requirements. Simultaneously, it will be found that in other regions, either because of technical efficiency or the vagaries of nature resulting in periodic droughts, total crop failures may be experienced, leading to famine. Today the allocation and distribution of the world's food supplies is still hopelessly inadequate, the position frequently being exploited for political purposes or for purely lucrative advantage. These food surpluses should be regarded as gifts of nature augmented by means of the knowledge and technology granted to certain more advanced or better equipped human beings, that they may serve as instruments for this purpose. Therefore, it is man's responsibility to see that these surpluses are fairly distributed and shared on an altruistic basis with those in greatest need and that no undue advantage should be taken of the destitute.

Furthermore, there still exist vast tracts of land in different parts of the world which are lying in an unproductive state notwithstanding their enormous potentialities with regard to food production. With the world's rapidly growing population, it is essential that the latent capacity of these relatively unproductive areas, which for the greater part are in the hands of less evolved nations, should be fully developed. However, this should not be achieved by any form of compulsion, or by economic or political exploitation, but by sharing technological and scientific knowledge through co-operation, prompting, guidance, encouragement and training of the indigenous population, thus gradually assisting to raise them to higher economic, technological and mental levels.

It is only in recent years that people have become more actively aware of the fact that the world's oceans, apart from their wealth of fish life, also contain tremendous possibilities for exploiting other biological resources such as micro animal and vegetable life, as well as mineral deposits found on the sea-bed. This is promising to be of major economic importance. During the past two decades, more specifically since 1967, a movement has been set afoot to have these resources internationalised by placing them under United Nations jurisdiction, thus seeking to have them recognised as belonging to humanity as a whole as well as to regulate their exploitation. No sooner had this movement been started, however, than it was confronted by various conflicting, selfish commercial and political interests from several nations, each trying to ensure the retention of a maximum share for their own purpose. One of the main limiting factors at present is that sea-fronting states, including all inhabited islands, claim jurisdiction over a coastal zone of sea of two hundred miles wide. At the present stage, prospects for arriving at a satisfactory solution for the just and impartial sharing of all ocean resources for the common good does not appear very promising with the spirit of greed and selfishness still rampant. For the final solution of this problem, it should be taken into consideration that there are countries which do not border on the seas at all, or otherwise only have a relatively limited sea frontage, whilst in other instances countries have a coast line out of all proportion with their size or population, or the comparative economic importance of the country. Consequently, it cannot be regarded as fair that countries which are not favoured with direct access to the sea should be largely or totally deprived of the right to share in the products of the seas. On the contrary, it should be arranged that the riches of the oceans must be available to all and shared proportionately either in accordance with the population or the genuine needs.

Sharing Knowledge

Over the ages mankind has systematically accumulated a vast stores of knowledge which, during the past century, has increased so rapidly that even the most intelligent human beings can at best assimilate and practically apply only a small part of that which is available. The result is that individuals, if they really wish to become expert in any specific field or interest, are forced to limit their attention or investigations to a relatively narrow terrain – to use the current expression, they have to specialise.

There are several shades of knowledge. To being with, knowledge may be considered as the sum-total of human experience and perception garnered in the past and reserved or stored for posterity through the channels of oral tradition or written records. With present day scientific developments some fantastic new devices for recording, storing, elaborating and recasting knowledge have been designed, especially with regard to the application of electronic principles and techniques in numerous forms of computers and recorders. A completely new science and industry has developed based on the effective application of these new principles.

The knowledge referred to above largely concerns that which has progressively been acquired by recording and correlating numerous facts in the brain – facts which originally were registered by the five physical senses. Such knowledge is subsequently absorbed, digested and finally transformed by the reasoning mind for practical application. But apart from this information, which might be classified as material or discriminative knowledge, there is also knowledge of a more subjective nature which might be called intuitive, which is in no way related to the senses but is obtained through several subjective channels. Such knowledge may be impinged upon the mind as "brain waves", as inspiration "out of the blue", or may be provided by some form of clairvoyance or clairaudience.

So many of the new ideas or discoveries with which scientists and thinkers are enriching the store of human knowledge are however not really the product of man's fertile brain, as many persons in their ignorance, arrogance or self-assurance would like to believe. No, what actually happens is that as a result of concentrated thought or meditation, they have consciously or unconsciously succeeded in contacting the celestial thought-reservoir or "raincloud of knowable things", representing an inexhaustible source of information provided on higher spheres for the use of mankind by ethereal Entities who are responsible for so many aspects of human progress. Without consciously being aware of it, these thinkers are merely serving as instruments of contact for gathering and relaying new ideas and information intended for the benefit of all mankind. In their selfishness and ignorance, these individual channels however often try to commercialise such knowledge by using it for purely personal advantage. Notwithstanding such temporary diversion or abuse, it will nonetheless eventually serve to amplify the aggregate stock of human information.

Finally, there is one more category that should be mentioned, which might be termed as spiritual knowledge. This is the inner or subjective knowledge granted to those individuals who have become aware of the duality of life and have discovered the Path of Return, who are systematically augmenting their knowledge of the hidden realms and tasting the joys of a spiritual thought-life by sustained aspiration, study, meditation and service of their fellow men. One of the most important facets of such service is to share acquired spiritual knowledge with others encountered along the path of life. However, newly gained information should first be well assimilated, developed and co-ordinated with existing knowledge. Otherwise, it might be found that sharing immature knowledge might readily lead to glamour and confusion or give rise to forms of presumption or conceit, as the injudicious aspirant in his enthusiasm may be inclined to force his still rather crude interpretations of the Truth onto the unready.

On the other hand, there should be no undue delay in sharing the acquired information, as maturity of knowledge is a most relative concept. No man can ever dispose of the Absolute Truth and the understanding of Truth should therefore remain subject to constant adaptation, change and growth. In any case, what the aspirant learns, and which subsequently becomes absorbed by the mind and incorporated in the thought-reservoir, will in the course of time appear to him as comparatively elementary, depending on his point of reference or the stage of development to which he, as his own assessor, has attained. While new facts are progressively being added to his ever accumulating store of information, such knowledge will always appear inadequate to the humble seeker, no matter what his stage of progress, in the light of the visions revealed to him by his ever expanding horizons of consciousness. Man should therefore start sharing that which is at his disposal at an early stage, thus not only learning the art of sharing, but thereby also providing an added stimulus for acquiring fresh knowledge and for constantly replenishing the available supply. It will be found that although there are always those who have already reached more advanced positions along the Path, there will simultaneously be even greater numbers still lagging behind who will be only too eager to share the 'elementary' knowledge being offered. It is only experience and inner discrimination that will teach the individual what to share, the best technique, the right time and place, as well as to whom his knowledge could be fruitfully presented.

The gaining of knowledge also increases the aspirant's responsibility. If the acquired knowledge is not shared by applying it with discrimination for the benefit of others, it is bound to result in some form of inner stagnation or what might be called intellectual indigestion, which often is reflected as an obstruction or disorder of some kind in either the emotional or physical systems. So again it remains a question of ding the middle way by discerningly and skilfully sharing the acquired and assimilated knowledge with fellow men and by not hoarding or selfishly applying it to personal advantage.

Today, a needy world is eagerly awaiting the guidance and spiritual help of those fortunate members of the community who have been blessed with a greater measure of Light, whether resulting from direct inspiration or an inner urge driving the aspirant towards dedicated study of available literature. This deeper knowledge of the subjective worlds accorded to man was never intended to be commercialised. On the contrary, it should be shared as widely and freely as circumstances will allow with those ready for its reception, without any attempt to translate its worth into terms of money to derive financial gain from its propagation.

Providing the Needs for Spiritual Work

There is no doubting the fact that if spiritual work is correctly motivated, selflessly approached with goodwill, discrimination and skill, then the wherewithal for realising these aims will unfailingly be forthcoming, often from the most unexpected sources. It is all a question of demand and supply, of invocation and evocation. By the correct approach to the Law of Demand, the door will be unlocked permitting entry into the universal Halls of Supply. For this purpose, the blind faith of the mystic may at times prove effective, but it is far better to clearly understand the underlying principles, thus ensuring that the correct procedures are applied for implementing the release of Divine Energy.

The worker should in the first instance lose sight of himself and of any form of personal advantage to be gained by his efforts. His attention should solely be focussed on that which he can give to his group or to his fellow men in general by making the most effective use of the equipment at his disposal. His one objective should be to provide and bestow generously those privileges of mind and matter with which he has been entrusted for the promotion of the common weal. If this is performed with the highest incentives, with discrimination, skill, love and understanding, it will be found that the necessary supplies will unfailingly be forthcoming and replenished.

Here it should perhaps be briefly pointed out that there are some schools of esoteric thought which are inclined to misconstrue these basic principles by proclaiming that man disposes over the "divine right to universal energies" and that these will be manifested by the enunciation of platitudes, by mystical affirmations or merely by claiming man's so-called inherent right of gratifying every supposed need as a divine privilege. These schools or individuals conveniently seem to forget that the favours so readily demanded or claimed, certainly are available and will definitely be bestowed under the right circumstances. What is so readily disregarded, however, is that these prerogatives should be earned by the incumbent by pure, selfless and invocative living, by persistent aspiration, by loving service to humanity and the Hierarchy and, finally, by sustained sharing of all that is so generously furnished.

Conclusion

In the foregoing passages the attention has been drawn to some of the many ways open to man for sharing the never ending range of gifts and energies with which Life has so generously provided him. If it could only be realised that each and every individual, whatever the position he occupies in life, whether rich or poor, whether high or low in social status or in intellectual attainments, has something of value that can be imparted and shared with his fellow men. In this connection it is interesting to note that those less abundantly blessed with worldly goods than their more affluent neighbours are often far more liberal in sharing that which happens to be at their disposal. But as a rule, people do not seem to be aware of the fact that of even greater importance than the sharing of material possessions, is that the whole being of the individual should be opened up to be permeated with the abundance of divine Love showered upon man from supernal levels. This appropriated energy then has to be shared readily, freely and with heart-felt understanding with all and sundry encountered along the Path of Life. In fact, the energies of Love, Goodwill and Understanding may be regarded as the most valuable single divine gifts that can be bestowed on man and there can hardly be any greater joy in life than to share these generously with fellow men.

A wonderful future lies in store for humanity, provided each individual contributes his fair share of positive and constructive energy in accordance with the position he occupies in time and space, as well as with the station attained on his evolutionary path. He must always remember that everything attained in life should be earned by applying the necessary effort or energy.

Those who are not in the position to personally provide public teaching or to write, should devise some other means of communicating and sharing their knowledge and thoughts with their associates.

Otherwise they could contribute of their time, money or facilities to enable others to serve and realise the plan more effectively and with greater rapidity.

There should always be the clear realisation that to build the coming New World, all forms of hatred, envy, selfish desire and competition should step by step be eliminated and substituted with selfless sharing of all that life on Earth is offering so abundantly and lavishly. As long as life remains characterised by extremes of riches and poverty, something is still seriously lacking in the ruling system of human association.

It is therefore not of great moment in what form or capacity man gives, as long as he gives liberally and without stint of that which is at his disposal, never forgetting that the greatest gifts that can be accorded are those arising from the heart as a result of closer contact with the Soul. Such gifts will therefore be steeped in Love, goodwill and understanding, leading to constantly improving human relationships and the eventual synthesising of all men into the ONE HUMANITY!

V

THE PATH OF RETURN

'Individualisation' and Evolution of Man

Ever since the 'individualisation' of animal-man or, in other words, when aeons ago certain highly developed animals were endowed with a spark or fractional part of the One Soul, thus becoming "ensouled" and thereby raised from the animal into the human kingdom, these components of mankind have remained in a constant process of evolution. Though this evolution in the first instance concerned the physical body, the closely associated emotional and mental bodies, all forming part of the personality, were progressively also involved.

Although the intangible, ephemeral bodies of the emotional and mental aspects of the personality are normally imperceptible to human senses, nonetheless, they are esoterically considered to be material and, in conjunction with the tangible physical body, to be of a transient nature, functioning only during the course of a single lifetime and disintegrating after the withdrawal of the soul and its attending life forces with the 'death' of the physical body. But notwithstanding this break in continuity, nature has proved the necessary techniques and suitable equipment to ensure that evolutionary gains acquired during the process of practical living in the three worlds of human experience are retained and preserved for posterity. This is effected by means of the chromosomes contained in the human reproductive cells, which are the carriers of individual characteristics and serve to transmit hereditary qualities of the personality from generation to generation. This carrying forward of acquired characteristics takes place on a selective but cumulative basis, thereby ensuring that the vehicle which must serve the soul as an instrument of experience is progressively adaptive and of suitable quality to fulfil the ever evolving demands of the indwelling spirit.

In man, spiritual evolution is achieved by means of what in human terms is known as the 'immortal' soul, using the physical vehicle as its apparatus of experience. At the end of a term of life the soul withdraws from the phenomenal body to return to its spiritual abode. The soul remains in these realms of spirit for a longer or shorter period until the urge arises for further experience in the world of matter. Then a new young body is sought in which to reincarnate – a body destined to function under circumstances more or less conforming to the soul's particular requirements for sustained unfoldment.

As already pointed out, primitive man was invested with a soul from earliest times since his manifestation as a human being, but for millennia during the course of innumerable incarnations, this spiritual presence remained unnoticed and totally obscured by the dominating physical aspects of the lower bodies. Nonetheless this inconspicuous soul, although still largely dormant as far as its direct influence on the material vehicle is concerned, avails itself of the provided opportunities by systematically abstracting and assimilating the essence from the experiences gained during these many lives passed in the world of matter.

Growing Illumination of the Soul

During the passing millennia the obscured soul slowly gathers energy and stature, until it gradually begins to manifest itself as a minute point of light. With succeeding incarnations this light steadily grows in strength and quality, until on occasion some of its beams are reflected and become discernible in the personality. And so the innate divine energy focussed in the soul grows from vigour to vigour, exerting an ever increasing influence over the personality, until for each evolving soul a life supervenes when it periodically begins to exercise a definite guiding influence on the integrated personality. This is the stage known in esoteric terminology as the Birth of the Inner Christ, marking the point of reverse in man's spiritual evolution and the phase where the awakening aspirant steps onto the Path of Return, the Path leading back to the House of the Father and back to the SOURCE.

Whether realised or not, the individual on the Path of Return is always a wielder of spiritual power. During the early stages the person concerned remains unaware of the powers with which he is increasingly being entrusted. This is probably just as well, as he is simultaneously granted the opportunity of gradually preparing himself for this privilege of gradually preparing himself of these new potencies with due humility, goodwill, love and understanding. But in spite of these qualities and at times actually because of the driving force engendered by achievements in serving his fellow men, the attitude and activities of the server are frequently misunderstood and misconstrued by his contemporaries. Such negative reaction and even scorn may be inspired by envy or malice, giving rise to actual repudiation of sincerely motivated, altruistic or even sacrificial service activities. However, notwithstanding such reverses, he will inevitably exert a growing influence on his environment and, depending on circumstances, even in the world at large.

Personality Integration and Identification with the Soul

The Path of Return is the stage when the emphasis is withdrawn from that which solely concerns outer manifestation. It indicates the phase when the concrete mind is step by step tuned in to the recognition and registration of conscious knowledge of the inner man, of that which is intangible and spiritual and which up till now has largely remained unknown – hidden behind the phenomenal façade and the glamoured mind. It is therefore the Path that leads from purely physical consciousness through various stages of emotional awareness to mental and finally spiritual consciousness. It is in the course of this process that the physical, emotional and mental bodies are systematically developed, eventually to be co-ordinated and fully integrated to function as a single unit – the conscious and vital personality – which now can serve as an effective instrument through which the soul can find expression and gain conclusive experiences. This is also the stage when the integrated personality, through the developing mind, becomes consciously aware of the presence of the soul. At first this results in the temporary illusion of duality, until the personality is slowly merged and closely identified with the soul, which from now on, as a soul-infused personality, can serve the Masters as a useful tool.

The dedicated aspirant is granted no respite. For him life consists of a never ending struggle towards self-improvement through the discipline, purification and refinement of the lower bodies, thus moulding them into an ever more reliable instrument of service. While these activities are progressively proceeding, the equipment involved must simultaneously be brought into practical service by applying it to maximum advantage to existing circumstances as determined by time and place, in accordance with the dispositions of destiny.

It is only through self-induced effort, relentless striving, sustained meditation and loving service of the fellow man that the path leading to perfection may be trodden. It is a lengthy and laborious path which, through experiment, experience and frequent temporary reverses or apparent failures, finally leads to success by teaching the incumbent to realise his objectives by the conscious and purposeful utilisation and manipulation of the energies always at his disposal, which oft need prior recognition.

The pilgrim on his way should be guided by the Inner Light, the Light of his own soul. This Light will begin by revealing to him his many limitations and undesirable characteristics to which he is still subjecting his world of outer contact. His inner radiance will thus accentuate the areas of darkness which still occur and have been retarding his progress, leading to those tides of deep depression and even despair – frequently typical expressions on the Path of the aspiring individual. Yet this is all for the good, as it is only by recognising the remaining shortcomings that they may be systematically opposed and overcome by persistent effort. By focussing the light in the head onto these areas of darkness, the clouds are gradually dispersed, thus introducing the clear light of day so that the inner sun can shine forth in all its glory.

The aspirant striving to follow the Path must learn to become aware of the dictates of the soul, in other words, he must adhere to and give expression to his highest interpretation of the Truth at that particular state of his development. When this procedure is consistently followed, it will automatically induce the manifestation of revelation after revelation, which will remain as beacons along his way of progress. The seeker of Truth should also cultivate an attitude of acceptance with a willingness to joyously endure those temporary hardships, pain and even agony which destiny may have in store for him, which apparently are essential for the continued shaping of his character to provide the correct approach to life. To reach his goal, he must learn to walk the middle path, first by recognising the pairs of opposites and then through discrimination and blending of these extremes to find the point of equilibrium.

Discrimination of the Real

In the struggle towards the new goal which the disciple is envisaging, the first problem is to free himself from the illusory panorama of the astral world by which the average person is constantly surrounded and controlled. To dissociate his own aura from this spurious and distorting surround will not only demand unrelenting and painstaking effort and self-discipline, but also discrimination. It is only through clear discernment by the analysing and evaluating mind that truth will be successfully distinguished from glamour, thereby bringing the astral nature under control, enabling the next step to be taken with greater confidence. Once the aspirant has received the first glimpse of the Light of Reality to be found beyond the receptive glamour of the astral plane, in other words, once he has become aware of the persistent call of his own soul, nothing will be able to hold him back or prevent his eventually progress towards his still elusive objective.

During man's advance along the Path the keynote of his vibrations is ever changing and constantly heightened as he himself climbs upward from cycle to cycle in a spiral process. The life of the active aspirant will therefore be qualified by an incessant series of experiences, revelations, changes and differentiations resulting from periodic construction, followed again by disruptions and subsequent reconstruction of the disrupted areas. It will thus be a life mingled with joy and pain, marked by the satisfaction and pleasure of achievement as well as the frustration and distress of failure resulting in apparently never ending suffering. The determined striver will however persevere in creating new ideals, only to find in due course that these are but intermediate stations along the upward Path, to be transcended in turn by ever more exalted objectives.

Furthermore, this adopted road will in many respects prove to be a lonely one, because each individual has to find his own specific way best suited to his particular character and combination of circumstances to which his rate of progress will have to be adjusted. And thus it will be found that so often old friends, associates or even loved ones are unable to understand him or keep pace with his development and are thus temporarily left behind, only to follow at a later stage at their own pace.

Obey the Silent Voice of the Soul

The walking of this Plan also demands a steady expansion of consciousness and therefore a corresponding increase in sensitivity to higher vibrations as well as obedience to the silent but insistent inner voice of the soul. This in turn will induce a dedication to motives which are constantly being raised to ever higher levels, as well as a growing fearlessness of the future and therefore a willingness to experiment in response to inner urging. This again will encourage a developing imagination and vision, which will have to be curbed by a well balanced mental approach and careful weighing of all relative evidence, thus ensuring sound discrimination. All these considerations can only be synthesised and brought to proper expression in an atmosphere created by purity of both thought-life and practical living.

Those who are considering the esoteric approach to life must be prepared for heavy demands in discarding or sacrificing aspects which thus far have been regarded as of major importance. On the other hand considerable rewards may be expected by walking this lonely path of the spirit, which each individual has to find and explore by personal effort, thus gaining increased independence, assuming fresh and larger responsibilities, and being better equipped for ever higher duties.

One of the first essentials for the man attempting to walk the Path of Return is that he must learn to adapt himself and to accept conditions as they happen to occur during the normal course of events. So often man is inclined to avoid or run away from circumstances, from inharmonious conditions and from problems which life has staged to serve as a challenge to test his mettle. By avoiding such provoking situations he is casting away opportunities which were granted him as stepping stones for more rapid progress. In confronting such outer conditions, it is imperative that his external attitude and reactions should be correct. Of even greater importance is that his inner motivations should be deliberately and consciously directed and established on the highest possible levels, that emotions should be guided by discrimination, tolerance, love and understanding. When ruled by these considerations every situation will be handled to maximum advantage, at the same time ensuring definite progress.

When the even flow of personality life is disrupted by pain and distress the inclination is, as a rule, to forget that such disturbances may actually serve as agents of release if correctly interpreted, understood and if met with suitable response. It may thus in fact prove to be just the experience needed for shattering the crystallised crust of glamour by which the personality has covertly been surrounded, and which has been retarding its development by preventing penetration of the energies of Love and Light. Man should therefore regard these apparent adversities rather as challenges and opportunities to break away from the established ruts and routines of life, thus enabling him to enter and explore fresh avenues of approach to the ever higher objectives that will be outlined by the soul. And if the upward climb proves to be stiff, hard and often lonely, then the struggler should realise that he is never really alone and that he can always depend on the silent but loving support of the spiritual presences who are constantly on guard and in contact with him on etheric levels and on whose steadfast help he can safely rely at all times.

Of the many qualities to which the disciple has to comply, which must constantly be developed or improved on his upward path, the most significant that can be singled out is surely the effective application of the Energy of Love. Actually this energy is so comprehensive that it cannot be adequately dealt with in the present theme. In fact, every thought should be motivated and founded on love of the fellow man, love of Nature, love of those Helpers of the spiritual spheres of whom he has become consciously aware and, finally, love of the Whole, of the ONE. It is not always sufficiently realised that the effective use of the Energy of Love and therefore its practical expression in the love of

Nature, can also be consciously and deliberately cultivated and stimulated by focussed attention, until in due course it will be expressed spontaneously as a radiant source of Light. Such a radiant beacon may then serve as an additional focal point for the further spreading of the energies of Light and Love to the rest of humanity, many of whom still remain in darkness, frozen and unawakened because of life's circumstances and the lacking warmth and comfort of Love. Ever more of these focal points of distribution of Light and Love are today urgently needed by our spiritual Brothers. May each and everyone becoming aware of these potential inner powers exert every effort to contribute their small share towards this combined endeavour!

Serve without Thought of Personal Gain

By increased concentration on the inner life, the power can be achieved not only to accede to the demands of daily life and normal human relationships, but also to function actively as a loving soul. It is the achieving of such dual existence that should form the disciple's principal objective, which eventually will result in a completely soul-infused personality, no longer interested in any form of personal gain or advantage, but solely concerned with serving humanity and promoting the exigencies of the Divine Plan as outlined by the Masters.

For the aspirant there are three main approaches which will facilitate walking the Path of Light. First of all, he will have to adjust himself to a life of loving service to his fellow men. It must be clearly understood however that such service should be motivated by a true spirit of goodwill and loving understanding and not by a disguised but selfish desire for personal reward or advancement. Secondly, the ascendancy of the soul over the personality will have to be encouraged by study and intellectual development, which will lead to a recognition and understanding of the pairs of opposites, thus enabling him to follow the 'narrow middle path' and to achieve true balance and the necessary discrimination to arrive at the correct decisions with regard to the many problems with which he will consistently be faced. And then lastly, the disciple must become a beacon of Light, because the Light he has gained must not only form his own guide to the primary Source of Light, but must simultaneously serve as a focal point of secondary light on behalf of younger brothers still struggling in the surrounding astral world of darkness and glamour.

The objective of the disciple should therefore be to train himself systematically in understanding and loving service of his fellow man in the circumstances where he has been placed by life and destiny, with the equipment at his disposal. This will be effected by sustained discipline of the lower nature and the discarding of those qualities which previously have been obscuring and impeding the unfolding soul nature, ultimately resulting in revelation and realisation.

When the struggle between the dualities on the mental plane has finally been concluded, with the victorious spiritual forces of the soul standing forth in clear command over the material and desire nature of the personality, the stage is reached where the disciple has lifted himself from the world of illusion in which he has immersed for aeons, to gain access into the ranks of the Elder Brothers. From now on, he will contribute his share with the deliberate wielding of forces for the realisation of the Divine Plan and in disciplining the elementals responsible for the creation of system and order out of confusion. This will become the objective of each individual who has the courage to tread this arduous Path. It is an opportunity lying in store for each and every aspirant willing to approach life's problems and struggles with discrimination and with the determination to overcome on their way, but always with the clear proviso that their initiative is prompted by selflessness, goodwill and loving understanding, and serve of their fellow human beings.

The dedicated disciple will eventually reach the stage when the Path of Light will lie clearly beaconed before him. Though it may again fade away into the mists of far horizons, he will no longer hesitate as to the direction to be followed, nor will he allow himself to be retarded anew by the glamours and obstructions of the astral world still holding the average man in bondage.

VI

ACCEPTANCE

The Purpose of Life

One of the main characteristics of the average man is his consistent search for a reasonable measure of peace, especially peace of mind. This is not only a feature of the present time with its apparently never ending tensions, disturbances and strife on all possible levels, but to a varying degree and under different circumstances, this must also have been typical of life during bygone ages.

In his attempts at attaining such peace and harmony, man is, however, rarely consciously aware of the fact that his reason for existing in the physical world is not in the first instance to lead a happy, quiet and relatively uneventful life, but to the contrary, that he has been born into this 'vale of tears' with the express purpose of gaining experience – experience of every possible form and nature. By extracting the essence from these trials, man is enriching his soul and ensuring its continued unfoldment. Therefore, a life of relative serenity should, from the broader point of view, be regarded as a life of wasted opportunity. Periods of temporary calm should however be welcomed as they provide short terms for recuperation and recovery of balance, for bringing gained experience into perspective, for appraising secured lessons and for restoring energy, before plunging again into further turmoils of life and renewed cycles of striving and experience.

For securing the maximum benefit from life's adventures, it is important that the aspirant should, as far as possible, acquire complete control over his emotional life. To realise this, one of his primary objectives should be to learn acceptance of that which destiny has in store for him. Here it must immediately be pointed out that, as with most words and expressions, several meanings may be attached to 'acceptance'. What is referred to in the present instance is certainly not a negative attitude of weak or indolent pusillanimity, of affable resignation to all that circumstances may provide, without displaying the stamina to stand up to and courageously face adverse conditions. No, acceptance as understood in the present theme refers to judicious acquiescence to those karmic conditions which man has evoked and brought upon himself either as a result of his current attitude to life or otherwise as a consequence of past activities. These effects now catching up with him and being brought to expression might be either favourable or un-favourable, depending on the nature of the originating cause.

In other instances such acceptance alludes to the broader aspects of the Divine Plan, which lie beyond personal control and are unfolding and taking their course, affecting all of humanity and creation, leaving the individual no choice but that of acceptance, whether he likes it or not. Therefore under these circumstances let the man conform with good grace, insuring that occurrences and conditions are used to best advantage, as each set of circumstances contains both its positive and negative aspects which can be turned to advantage when correctly handled.

Acceptance is the Key

So the key to a future life of increased light, vision, expansion of consciousness and of service, lies in acceptance, whereby the aspirant will inevitably attract to himself fresh experiences, leading to further tests, increased responsibilities and ever greater inspiration and Light. Such acceptance and subsequent increased activities will unavoidably also be attended by sacrifice, eventually however definitely leading to serenity and joy. Should the worker on the other hand avoid or reject true recognition of and submission to ruling circumstances, conditions or occurrences, this would mean the negation and discarding of opportunities and challenges which might have served to stimulate him to enhanced goodwill, consciousness, group relations or service, which would have meant taking another step along the Lighted Way to greater selflessness and a deeper penetration into the subjective world of spirit. Instead, desperate opposition to and fanatic struggling against inevitable destiny can only result in frustration, pain and misery and also in lost time and opportunity.

The only way to redemption and liberation therefore lies along the path of acceptance and thus of sacrifice, these two concepts being largely synonymous. Therefore, do not hesitate to bring any sacrificial offerings that may be demanded, because it is by this means that the disciple will be led from selfishness to the renewed light of redemption, to joy, reality and Life Eternal!

To begin with, the aspirant must come to terms with himself, learning for the time being to accept his own shortcomings, faults and limitations, but certainly not resigning himself to these conditions. Recognition followed by acceptance of these restrictive influences will prove an essential step in countering them and in working for their redemption. For this purpose, one of the first requirements will be a detached approach and strict impersonality, this permitting a selfless and impartial evaluation of the personality and objective discernment of the procedures required for their amelioration and eventual subjugation. Once the aura is permeated with a spirit of acceptance, it provides a field of energy and of potential creative and expansive quality that will serve to thwart emotional conflicts, thus relieving personality tensions of fear, anxiety, desire and reactivity.

The life of the aspiring human being is not an easy one and acceptance of unavoidable karmic events and circumstances, whatever their origin, is essential. What this really amounts to is acceptance of the Divine Plan and subsequent collaboration with this Plan, instead of detrimentally opposing it with the free will and personality decisions. Wherever there is rejection, such released and unrestrained energies tend to disturb the smooth unfoldment of the over-all pattern, thus contributing towards disrupting the effective functioning of the Plan. The aspirant is thereby also obscuring his own light, impeding his Path and creating the illusion that it is unduly rough and cluttered with barriers, hampering progress and making it unnecessarily painful.

Right Understanding, Sound Discrimination and True Activity

A growing tendency towards discriminative acceptance is also an indication that the aspirant is learning the secret of duality, that he is finding himself between the pairs of opposites, the personality and the soul and that he is seeking the way out. He is therefore moving from the probationary path on to that of discipleship and is consciously becoming engaged in that long and arduous battle on the astral plane wherein control over the emotional and desire life has to be gained. It is only by acquiescence that the emotional aspects of the personality can gradually be brought into accord with the divine objectives of the indwelling soul. This should not assume the form of a negative and weak submission to superior forces, the so-call Will-of-God, but should in the first instance be demonstrated by unflinching recognition of the relative position attained, followed by a positive approach to the manifested conditions or events. For such confident procedure, the disciple should devote the powers at his disposal to best advantage endeavouring to achieve right understanding and sound discrimination, which must then lead him to true activity. The trouble is, however, that so often instead of adopting a firm and positive attitude and making the best of circumstances, the individual will fall into that dreadful illusionary state of self-pity becoming so occupied with himself and his largely self-inflicted or imaged suffering, that he loses all sense of balance and perspective, finally landing himself into the very depths of affliction and misery. In contrast, the next man will avail himself of the positive aspects of the same conditions, seeing them as proffered opportunities, thus succeeding in advancing some further steps along the Way and experiencing the joys of an ever expanding consciousness and an unfolding world of Light.

Although man as a rule is not consciously aware of the fact, there are actually three closely related and interacting fundamental principles on which judicious acceptance will be founded. These are Impersonality, Detachment and 'Divine Indifference'.

Impersonality

Acceptance infers in the first instance true recognition of circumstances and of reality, and subsequently learning the very difficult lesson of achieving an impersonal and detached approach and as an impartial observer acquiring the faculty of studying and weighing all the facts related to the position, always remembering that genuine impersonality can only be based on love and real understanding and should therefore be exercised with complete self-forgetfulness.

For the cultivation of true impersonality, it is first of all essential that all selfish desire, ambition and craving for power should be eliminated from the threefold lower man. This will demand the courage of conviction, persistence and the power to stand steady and to handle every situation in a spirit of love – thus eventually leading to a calm and unhurried consideration of all the factors and circumstances influencing a given situation – this in turn being inductive to discriminative conclusions. Disciples will, however, find that it is most difficult to maintain such an impersonal attitude under all circumstances. This will particularly be the case when man has to take stock of himself and when cherished ideas, hard won qualities and carefully nurtured concepts have to be reconsidered and adapted; at times these will even have to be radically changed or altogether rejected as a result of new light secured and the effect of intuitive inspiration. That complete impersonality has not yet been achieved, is often apparent when the disciple is still hungering for recognition of the service he is rendering or when he is frustrated because of the lack of public reaction evidenced to the light he is trying to kindle and to spread to his fellow men. These are all aspects which the true server must learn to accept with impersonality, indifference and equanimity.

The first step towards achieving spiritual love and real understanding of others, is to maintain a balanced impersonality in all personal dealings. This will lead to a consciousness illumined by the clear light of the intuition, thereby opening the 'window of vision' to spiritual spheres, overcoming the obstructions and distortions of the astral plane and recognising the reality of the many aspects of all life and form.

Contrary to the opinion invariably entertained by those left behind on the path of spiritual development, the impersonality evidenced by the advancing disciple is not based on apathy or preoccupation, but is actually engendered by a deeper understanding of reality. It is founded upon a sound sense of proportion, the energy of the will-to-good, a dynamic urge to serve and a detachment which facilitates the bestowing of true help where and when it is needed. In practice, this means the elimination of impeding sentiment or those emotional reactions of liking and disliking, which often constitute such important and disturbing factors in personal or group relationships.

Detachment

The secret governing appropriate acceptance is not only an impersonal approach to problems and circumstances, but such impersonality should be qualified by discrimination and detachment. The worker should cultivate the attitude of a silent observer, without undue identification with that which it is hoped to attain. The principle of silence should furthermore be stressed, because so often the objective fails to be realised because of ill-advised and premature speech.

This implied detachment should be of a mental nature, allowing the thinker to avoid the numerous snares of the emotions by raising the thoughts to the less disturbed and more peaceful regions of the mind, from which the proposed task can then be promoted with confidence. Therefore, learn to stand emotionally detached, achieving this by acceptance, loving understanding and, finally, by spiritual attachment. Learn to practise that detachment which will enable the worker to live as a soul in the sphere of his daily activities! Learn that there is no occasion for criticism between spiritual workers, as this only leads to obstruction of the work! Learn to accept fellow workers as they are, to supersede the tendency towards pronounced likes and dislikes by not focussing the attention on the many petty existing or imagined shortcomings so typical of each individual character, which have their roots in the ephemeral nature of the personality – against which each disciple is waging his own private battles and which in due course will be overcome and eliminated! Yes, all this can be achieved by detached acceptance.

Owing to the nature of his work, the average disciple is unavoidably brought into constant association with both fellow workers and the public in general. To accomplish his obligations effectively, his only sound approach will be to maintain a spirit of subjective detachment, which will then lead him to understanding, acceptance and smooth collaboration in that united effort which is so essential for ensuring greater spiritual enlightenment for the world at large.

It should always be kept in mind that by accepting the many vagaries of man and of life in general, a considerable contribution can be made in bringing the turbulent waters of astral levels to repose and serenity, thus rendering them sensitive to impressions from the soul or from higher instances and clarifying the vision for clearer discernment of the soul's objectives.

Life consists of a continuous range of activities and experiences, which are in fact the opportunities presented by destiny. These experiences may often be the source of acute suffering, but it is through such suffering that life's lessons are most readily learnt once the worker reaches the stage of detachment and acceptance. In the course of his work, the disciple should, however, be careful not to identify himself unduly with the problems, emotions and suffering of those he is entrusted to help, because he can actually render far more effective service by remaining detached and uninvolved – not as a form of self-protection, which would of course be the selfish attitude, but to retain his balance and perspective for more adequate service. A true appraisal of those to be helped can only be made by a detached approach – accepting them as they are with both their apparent faults and their virtues, their divine qualities and utterly human attributes – then subjecting them to the all-encompassing power of love.

The aspirant should therefore learn to practise inner or spiritual detachment from the clamouring demands of those encountered on the astral levels of the Path of Life, thus releasing the mind to increased intuitive perception. At the same time he should not neglect acceding to those commitment for which he already has assumed responsibility in the world of material affairs. This will, however, involve a complete readjustment of the values and activities of the material life to the demands of the soul. It is only through selfless detachment, judicious acceptance and the pouring forth of love and understanding, that man will learn to find his true balance and to stand in spiritual being whilst simultaneously contriving to provide adequate and potent service to those still bound to material conditions.

Furthermore, for ready acceptance the disciple must also acquire the art of total relinquishment and renunciation or, in other words, complete identification with the soul. Once he has learned to release the hold of all desires of the personality, he then stands free to accept all that life has to offer, since such acceptance will no longer be for the satisfaction of the lower vehicles, but for the re-channelling and distribution of the bounties and energies of supernal origin to those points where they are needed.

'Divine Indifference'

Finally, acceptance may also find expression by an attitude which the Tibetan has so aptly termed 'Divine Indifference'. This is the 'don't care' attitude which disregards anything tending to produce pain or other forms of severe emotional reaction in any of the personality vehicles. Such reactions should merely be registered and then endured, tolerated and eventually ignored, whilst the disciple concentrates his attention with patience, forbearance, goodwill and loving understanding on his duties and service activities. This form of indifference to outer events is qualified as 'divine' to distinguish it from cold and detached separativeness from an attitude of casual aloofness or of being unconcerned. It is therefore the attitude which accepts circumstances as they present themselves and then makes the best of them, not allowing the less favourable aspects to carry undue weight, or to gain the upper hand. Actually, it is the attitude maintained by the soul towards the threefold lower bodies, rejecting all that is expressive of selfish desire and other negative or traditional personality characteristics of the past. This 'divine indifference' can, however, only be attained by first of all purging the mind of all that is critical and unkind and then superseding these with love, goodwill and understanding.

With successful introduction of 'divine indifference', emotions and ancient glamours that have been impeding spiritual development, will gradually die of attrition and fade out because they are no longer acknowledged and supported. Such gaining of emotional control must be regarded as constituting one of the most important single steps in the spiritual progress of the aspirant.

This spiritual indifference, leading to acceptance of all that life has in store, will also result in negating that adverse inclination towards intense self-interest still so evident in the average person during his earlier stages of awakening, and which inevitably has a tremendous retarding effect until it can be mastered or superseded. It will finally allow the soul to stand free, unattached and in complete control of the personality.

Therefore, in conclusion, it can be said that for unreserved acceptance, true understanding and effective service, the disciple should be characterised by an impersonal and detached approach to life, qualified by an attitude of 'divine indifference' to the claims of the personality. This signifies achieving a neutral attitude towards the demands of the threefold lower bodies constituting the not-Self, and a refusal to become unduly identified with anything except the highest spiritual reality to which the individual can attain at his stage of development, thus allowing the devoted aspirant to become the inspired and dedicated Server.

VII

HUMILITY

Today there are thousands of individuals throughout the world within whom the Inner Christ has already been born, who are evidencing this fact by dedicated aspiration, a spontaneous tendency for expressing goodwill, an attitude of loving understanding towards fellow men and an affinity for the spiritual values of life. Whether realised or not, large numbers have definitely entered the Path of Return. Consequently, they are consistently being subjected to the numerous trials and tests, temptations and pitfalls normally encountered along the Way. It is only through the gaining of experience by having to choose between presented alternatives and eventually arriving at the right decisions, that man learns to distinguish between good and evil and to recognise Life's inherent opportunities, thereby gradually gleaning the essence from manifested existence.

Mean between Extremes

Amongst the many attributes by which man is qualified, that of arrogance or its inverse, an inferiority complex, can be daily observed. During the normal course of life, the individual is inclined to deviate unduly to either the one of the other of these extremes. However, both should be avoided by following the 'middle way' of humility. The latter condition may be achieved by approaching issues with a proper sense of proportion and balance, by avoiding all forms of emotionalism and by weighing available evidence with calm discrimination. The greatest danger lurks in an over-arrogance. Inevitably, such presumption is bound to come to a fall.

Arrogance is a child of ignorance, a product of myopic, faulty or unbalanced perception, confounded by the effects of dwelling in the glamours of the physical and astral worlds. Arrogance is the condition of the person whose interests are still largely focussed in matter, who is inflated with the conceit and self-esteem of success in gaining mastery over various physical aspects and in wielding certain powers on the confined material plane. Such individuals are only to be pitied. Their condition clearly indicates that they have not become aware of the limitations of their narrow sphere of activity nor have they awakened to the grandeur of the spiritual realities by which they are surrounded and of which matter is but the lowest manifestation. Such arrogance should therefore be recognised as a temporary phase in the unfoldment of the individual. The time will arrive, either in this life or another, when he will become conscious of the more profound values of existence. He will then be illumined by the Light of Truth and filled with deep humility at the realisation of his relative insignificance in the greater Whole. His new-found sense of proportion and therefore of humility, will henceforth be retained perpetually, and to whatever altitudes his unfoldment might ultimately reach, he can only be led to an ever clearer conception and appreciation of the unbounded immensity of the Universe and his own comparative inanity.

In contrast with the man of arrogance, the person suffering from an inferiority complex wastes his opportunities by not recognising his inherent capabilities. He fails to realise that these are the keys which will unlock the doors to fresh revelations, increased knowledge and experience and new avenues of service. A well balance point of view, a dispassionate and candid consideration of his abilities, faculties and natural gifts, is essential if the aspirant is to arrive at a true assessment of his potentialities and spiritual responsibilities. By unduly disparaging his attainments and attributes, he negates the powers of his own soul, thereby neglecting proffered opportunities and a true source of guidance. Therefore by all means walk humbly along the Path of spiritual living, but take care not to focus the attention unduly on either existing or imagined shortcomings. Certainly remain well aware of such imperfections and consistently work at their elimination, but there should simultaneously be a recognition and appreciate of the many gifts and graces with which the soul has endowed the personality, and which should be applied to the maximum benefit of mankind.

Another danger which lies concealed in an unjustified belittling of the self is that it actually amounts to the comparing of personal aptitudes with the supposed superior qualities of others. Such an approach may readily lend itself to the development of spiritual jealousy or, under certain circumstances, towards an inclination to obtrude the personality of others to attract attention.

It is, however, the self-opinionated comparison of acquired faculties or mental achievements with the accomplishments of others which so readily gives rise to forms of arrogance and, depending on circumstances, finds expression in presumptuous ideas with regard to status, prestige, achievement, intellect or knowledge. Yes, "comparisons are odious".

However, it is the power afforded by the wielding of money which above all is inclined to encourage arrogance. How little do these proud and over-bearing people realise that they are living in a fool's paradise of glamour! Their vanity is based on worldly possessions and accomplishments of a temporary and evanescent nature, which will be lost, if not before, then at the end of a fleeting physical life! In contrast, spiritual gains are garnered by the soul, not only for its own permanent enrichment and unfoldment, but for its transmutation into Light to be shed upon younger souls.

A Balanced Sense of Values

It is only when man comes to the realisation that he forms an inherent and intimate part of a greater Whole, of the One Humanity, and that his purpose in life should not be solely directed towards self-advancement to the detriment of others, that he becomes aware of a new sense of values. He then awakens to the need for a new and selfless approach to life wherein the powers at his disposal are applied primarily in service of his fellow men. Only when this stage is reached with arrogance and selfish concern be superseded by the humility of dedicated and selfless service. This worthy motivation is engendered by cultivating an inner detachment without entertaining any thoughts on the significant of the accomplished task. Humility, therefore, is the total ignoring of the self and the concentrating of all available energy towards the effective rendering of altruistic duty.

Although the disciple should be on constant guard against self-indulgence and self-centredness, periodically a certain degree of objective self-analysis remains essential. There are for instance disciples of retiring and self-effacing nature who display no trace of arrogance. Their problem is rather the conquering of a proneness towards self-deprecation, which must not in any way be confused with true humility. A disciple should learn to appraise his position on the Path with detachment and discrimination. For this purpose, humility should be joined with spiritual self-respect and a clear recognition of the spiritual status already attained. Excessive self-disparagement undermines the potential and effective work of a disciple, for, it is only by recognising his own powers and capacities that they may be wielded to full effect. However, such recognition should remain a strictly personal concern. After balanced consideration and self-assessment, the disciple should accept his personal appraisal with complete reticence, then proceeding to apply the identified attributes under the guidance of his soul to the task on hand. Therefore, forget about the urges of the personality! Keep on working and striving and serve with a joyous heart!

Unfoldment of Spiritual Humility

As the disciple advances along the Path, there will increasingly be a spontaneous development of his spiritual humility. The greater his success in dissipating the mists and glamours of the astral world which enshroud him, the clearer will be the outlines of the world of spirit revealed to his probing vision. Coupled with these expansions there will also be a growing awareness of his own relative insufficiency and insignificance in the greater Scheme. It will be found that sincere humility is an attribute of every true spiritual leader, for he is only too well aware of his own relative inadequacy with regard to the dimensions of the task he is undertaking.

Humility is the state of consciousness in which the personality is being brought under the direction of the soul when the glamours of the astral plane are dispelled by the powers of the mind and superseded by the Light of Truth. It is the phase when the disciple learns to face and evaluate the freshly revealed verities of life with calmness and dispassion. This inevitably leads him to a realisation and recognition of past errors and an acknowledgement of mistaken points of view which gave rise to false pride and arrogance.

The humble worker will evince no tendency towards aggressiveness in thrusting himself to the foreground. Rather will he quietly proceed along the path unfolding before his awakening vision as he steadily performs those self-initiated duties for which time and circumstance have qualified him. Although to the casual observer such work may seem to be of a simple nature, its inner effects may eventually prove far more potent and lasting than spectacular achievements performed with considerable fanfare and outer display. What is of decisive importance is whether such activities are selflessly motivated and performed with goodwill and loving understanding.

VIII

DOUBT AND SELF-CONFIDENCE

Every normal person is at times assailed with doubts of some nature. This is only to be expected, because each individual is equipped with a reasoning and enquiring mind which, depending on his stage of development and the circumstances to which he has been subjected by the fortunes of life, will be used more or less effectively for probing the innumerable problems with which he is daily confronted.

At the same time he becomes faced with the dilemma that he is relatively poorly equipped for registering and forming a true picture of the multiple forces by which he is constantly surrounded and which determine his circumstances. As it is, the average man merely depends on his five senses for observing and gauging his environment, and as a rule this will only enable him to distinguish his physical surround, leaving him totally unaware of that which is more ephemeral. Fortunately there are those who today are beginning to realise that the material realm only represents the lowest or crudest aspect of seven spheres of existence, these other worlds being of a more etheric or spiritual nature. It should furthermore be remembered that the senses cannot even register all of the physical world, and that subject to variations between the capacity of individuals, man's powers of observation are limited to only a relatively narrow range of vibrations which will determine his sphere of material recognition.

It is this relative inadequacy of man's sentient powers which, mostly unconsciously, gives rise to his many forms of doubt which subsequently so often find expression as various kinds of fear.

Doubt, in its many forms of manifestation, may therefore be considered to be an inseparable element of human existence. It first of all becomes apparent in those juvenile stages when consciousness becomes evident, remaining with the individual until awareness begins to fade, towards the termination of the physical life on earth.

Doubt forms an unavoidable part of all human existence, and is already present from early youth, remaining in constant attendance until the last moments of conscious physical being. It so often catches one unawares, stealing upon the individual like a thief in the night. Doubt encroaches when decisions have to be taken, and after failure, returns with redoubled power.

Our common-sense, penetrating self-search and reasoning, so often lead us to certain conclusions. When these personal inferences and views are, however, compared with those of others, they may be found to be at variance, resulting in doubts, inner conflicts and uncertainty as to right and wrong and this consequently leads to anxiety.

There are many disadvantages attached to hesitancy and doubts, but on the other hand it may at times also prove to be the evidence of a guiding hand drawing our attention to better alternatives, and gradually leading the reasoning and considering mind to higher objectives.

It will eventually be found that everything that is achieved by mental processes, having in the course of formulation passed through stages of vacillation and doubt, during which various considerations have been weighed against each other. Doubt is therefore an intermediate phase while the effect of various factors, facts and evidences are being counter-balanced. The trouble is, however, that some people are inclined to linger unduly in this state of uncertainty, apparently being unable to arrive at conclusive decisions.

Although a certain degree of doubt is indicative of, and therefore a characteristic of a questing mind, searching for that which is better and higher, it should at the same time not be allowed to undermine, sap or destroy man's ideals and objectives.

During the earlier stages of his development, man is inclined to follow blindly the course set, or the ideals pointed out to him by parents or teachers, until, after due experience and growing knowledge the individual mind progressively matures and begins to formulate its own ideas and arrives at its own decisions. There are, however, those who retain immature minds for the rest of their physical existence, remaining relatively free from plaguing doubts, because they rarely think for themselves, being satisfied to follow the path indicated by others. It is only with the awakening of independent thought, when different possibilities are weighed against each other, that doubt begins to arise, which when correctly handled, will serve to solve the problems.

There are of course those strong-willed, self-assured people who seldom seem to experience doubt, but who at the same time are often inclined to make serious mistakes because of over-confidence and ill-considered decisions.

Self-Confidence

Anyone wishing to achieve something worthwhile must rid himself of the negative and destructive effects of doubt and fear, and supersede these with a certain degree of self-confidence. A person without sufficient self-reliance can never attain his higher objectives, and remains merely a piece of flotsam tossed about on the stormy waters of daily living. Although such self-reliance, combined with boldness and courage, is an essential characteristic of the successful striver, the problem remains of truly directing available energy, because self-confidence can so easily degenerate into conceit, forgetting that the source of valour does not in the first instance lie within ourselves, but is proved from Higher Levels.

Lack of confidence makes one weak and ineffective, and leads to an inferiority complex and concern, whereas self-confidence, suitably directed, provides the necessary power to achieve the higher objectives that are being envisaged. This not only holds for material objectives, but applies in like measure to that which is exalted and spiritual.

When work is undertaken on behalf of fellow men and without selfish motivation, then, however difficult such a task might appear, self-assurance will enable the aspirant to tackle it with confidence and the reliance that the needed support from spiritual levels will be forthcoming. This, in most instances, will lead to a successful conclusion and the joy of realising that a further undertaking on behalf of others has been effectively accomplished, and that another step has been taken along the path of destiny. But the realisation must always be there that the power of achievement was granted by the Father, and furthermore that no demands will ever be made of the faithful worker which cannot be fulfilled.

Therefore have confidence in your life struggle. Have confidence that notwithstanding all the fears, obstacles and hardships which are bound to be encountered, these will finally be surmounted successfully. These difficulties should in fact be regarded as opportunities which have been offered, because the overcoming of such hurdles will serve as effective stepping stones for progressive spiritual unfoldment. Therefore systematically try to eliminate every form of doubt and anxiety, and above all learn to rely on the Love of God, which can always be depended upon, provided one's share of effort is faithfully contributed by consistently striving to accomplish the good with the light at one's disposal.

Actually true 'self'-confidence is merely a synonym for 'soul'-confidence. It is the unconscious, or in some instances even the conscious process of subjecting the activities of the physical instrument to the dictates of the higher Self or Soul, and if these inspirations are faithfully complied with the final results of such efforts are bound to prove beneficial.

Therefore pray for self-confidence, because without this you cannot serve as a child of the Father. Pray that you may never be deprived of this self-reliance, because without it you will be reduced to futility and insignificance – a material body without inspiration or power. Pray to the Father for support and strength to lead you to wisdom, power, love, and the self-assurance to apply these effectively for the benefit of humanity as a whole.

IX

STANDING ALONE

The Illusion of Spiritual Loneliness

What in current speech is known as loneliness usually refers to plights of the personality wherein the individual, as a result of personal attitudes, speech, activities or other inadequacies, finds himself maladjusted to his social environment. The present study often founded on either self-assertion or self-pity, for they can only be rectified by personal discipline with regard to established norms of social conduct. It alludes rather, to professed spiritual loneliness, which may be seen as a prevailing illusion or glamour which is apt to thwart the progress of the aspirant by impairing his vision.

The dedicated worker may at times feel lonely and forlorn because in his spiritual unfoldment he has outgrown his erstwhile associates, many of whom have consequently deserted him. Nonetheless, he knows that he is never really alone. He is merely exchanging some of his temporary fair-weather friends for those with whom he has already long-standing bonds, their links having been only temporarily obscured during his brief immersion in matter to gain some further experience. In many instances these old and trusted friends on 'the other side' may not as yet be clearly discernable. However, their presence will progressively be sensed more distinctly by those whose perception is developing and their unfailing support may be depended upon whatever the state of worldly conditions. Once conscious contact with this inner fraternity has been established, all forms of loneliness will automatically fade into oblivion.

The Solitary Path

In many respects the Path of Return is a lonely way. Those who have entered it, especially those engrossed in esoteric training who are on a pilgrimage to discover more about the hidden verities of life, should take into account that in essence this is a solitary path full of pitfalls and obstructions and demanding many sacrifices. Nevertheless, if this Path is trodden with sincerity and dedication, the compensations to be gained by eventual success will be beyond all expectation.

As a rule, this loneliness is one of the first impediments encountered on the Path and this the aspirant must be prepared to endure. Though the seeker may be surrounded by thousands following the same course, he will nonetheless have to clear his own individual path, surmounting the provided obstacles by his own personal efforts. He must therefore be prepared to meet hindrances and dangers of every nature, which provide the means of testing his tenacity and perseverance. The conquering of these obstacles will engender the required courage and confidence for tackling and overcoming the next hurdle that is sure to lie ahead. At the same time these crowned efforts will also bring the aspirant a joy of accomplishment and the knowledge and satisfaction of having advanced another step on the spiritual ladder.

If the disciple hopes to contribute his modest share to the Hierarchical Plan, he must firstly become sensitive to the outlines of the Plan. To achieve this, it is essential that he develop a condition of inner calm and detachment. It is only by inner solitude that the personality becomes receptive to the silent voice of the soul. This enables the secret faculties and powers of the Higher Self to function effectively through the soul to the mind from where the idea is subsequently transmitted to the brain for eventual physical expression. Solitude ensures that serenity of the soul which is needed if the Master is to impress his wishes concerning the outlines of the work to be accomplished, as well as the knowledge and techniques required for its fruition.

As man develops spiritually, he moves onto increasingly higher vibrations, not only functioning on such vibrations, but also radiating them to his environment. In practice this implies that he is raising his vibrations above those of his former surroundings. Consequently, it is not surprising that he grows out of tune with his associates, which readily leads to many forms of discord. The aspirant thus enters a period of self-imposed isolation, since his spiritual unfoldment brings an automatic breaking off of former relationships. Meanwhile, his vibration as yet does not synchronise with that of the spiritual group to which he is ascending. He is therefore standing midway between the outer world of matter and the inner world of spirit! He has broken with the past, but is yet uncertain of the future! This may give rise to a temporary feeling of utter loneliness.

By his spiritual development the aspirant becomes detached and lifted above the mass consciousness with which he used to be merged in the past, and which had largely determined his outlook and activities. As yet, however, he has failed to achieve firm connections with the group into which he will eventually be assimilated by conscious collaboration. There are those who at times may obtain a fleeting glimpse of that which is awaiting them, but in the beginning it will only be of a passing nature, only serving to accentuate their loneliness when the accorded vision fades away. The aspirant must therefore realise that, notwithstanding his progress, he has not yet wholly succeeded in extricating himself from the astral tentacles holding him back and obscuring his vision and consciousness. There is only one way to shed these fetters and dispel the illusions of loneliness – that is to persist whole-heartedly with his exertions, studies, meditation and devoted service of his fellow men. It will be found that faithful perseverance with these efforts will lead to the gradual disappearance of all forms of self-interest. His loneliness will be forgotten or disregarded to the same extent that his attention is being absorbed in the several facets of his service to others.

The aspirant student of the Ancient Wisdom teachings comes across many apparent paradoxes as he endeavours to apply the relative principles to practical living. Although his normal inclination may for instance be of a retiring nature, attempts at sharing his acquired knowledge with others will inevitably bring him into close and constant association with people beyond his usual circle of friends and acquaintances. On the other hand, for effective work he needs a spirit of real detachment, as the inclinations of the personality should not be allowed to force themselves unduly on the worker's activities or objectives. This refers in particular to the emotional body because for successful work an astral body will be needed that is sensitive to impress from both the soul and the Master. This can only be achieved if that body is kept relatively detached and reasonably free from emotional storms and problems, thus becoming serene, receptive and responsive. Therefore, the correct balance has to be found between the required social activities and spiritual detachment and isolation, always keeping in mind that the Lighted Way is in essence a lonely way.

At some stage or other each worker will be called upon by his own inner being to render service commensurate with the circumstances under which he finds himself. It will depend on his sensitivity whether this call will be met with recognition, correct interpretation and suitable response. Apart from the outward effect of such activities of service, there will be a corresponding inward reaction inducing spiritual growth. For maximum effect in this regard, it is important that the server should stand alone for arriving at his own decisions and that he should follow his own line of approach in executing the set task in accordance with the dictates of the soul. These inner instructions can only be communicated and recorded when the emotional body is in a state of harmony and tranquillity and therefore of relative detachment or isolation. This certainly does not preclude group work, which forms an important aspect of all future esoteric activity. However, before the disciple can effectively fulfil his group obligations, he has to attain the correct inner orientation which enables him to stand alone. As the worker advances along the Path of Light, every form of personal isolation will be negated step by step as individual identify becomes increasingly merged and identified with the Whole.

Instinctive reticence and relative aloneness is the normal condition of many aspirants on the Path of Discipleship. However, care should be taken that this does not inhibit the sharing of knowledge, experience and the resulting Light with fellow seekers on the Path or with younger brothers still lagging behind and who have not yet awakened to the beauty of that which lies in store for them.

One of the responsibilities of a disciple is to relieve affliction and suffering wherever possible in the world of pain and distress. However, it must always be remembered that it is often through the vehicle of pain and suffering that man learns the lessons which will determine his progress. Therefore never hesitate to give love and understanding, but at the same time it should be done with discretion. Others should not be deprived of the opportunity of personally solving the problems with which they have been confronted by destiny. They should be allowed to stand on their own feet and fight their personal battles in relative solitude. By utilising the powers at their disposal, they will be able to advance another step on their strenuous path of progress and become better equipped for surmounting the inevitable obstructions still to be encountered in the future. There are therefore occasions when true love has to stand aside, whilst looking on with pain, though nonetheless with compassion and understanding, as loved ones fight their battles in comparative loneliness. This enables them to learn to stand on their own feet and gain the needed experience of life.

'Esoteric Solitude'

Every aspirant will eventually reach the stage which might be called 'esoteric solitude'. This phase does not refer to attitudes or activities, but to the attainments of the soul. Therefore, while a man's personality may take part in various social functions and maintain many friendships, only a few of his associates will be able to share the inner peace achieved at his spiritual pinnacle. The latter is represented by his point of entry into the world of spirit, where contact is made with his future associates. Only a few of those still bound by the glamours of the world of matter will be able to follow him. However, if such a state is to prevail as a normal attribute of his life, it will demand his conscious withdrawal from the usual round of social enterprises thus enabling him to serve his environment as a more effective channel for the expression of love, understanding and radiant living.

Yes, generally speaking, the Path of Return remains a lonely one. It is to be trodden by each aspirant according to his own particular life pattern as determined by the various Rays of Energy to which he is subjected, and in accordance with the karma evoked as a result of his own past actions. In addition there are also the many facets of human and world karma over which he exercises no control and, finally, there are the dictates of his own soul. This lonely Path which may be shared in varying degree with fellow travellers, may in rare instances prove to be of unmitigated joy. For the majority of individuals it will however, be a path of sacrifice and of outer pain and suffering, but these trails will as a rule be amply rewarded by an inner joy of spiritual achievement. This solitary path may often lead to scorn and ridicule from unenlightened bystanders who as yet lack under- standing and the realisation that it will also be their destined road at some later stage of life. It is finally a solitary path qualified by persistent self-discipline, where the aspirant has to learn to stand alone on his own feet, quietly and self-confidently carrying on with his self-appointed task of serving his fellow men to the best of his ability. Let him not be dissuaded by any form of temporary rejection, misunderstanding or even abuse from those still lacking vision and consciousness, from those not realising the illusion and the futility of all selfish striving, of satisfying the lusts and desires of the personality and of all other forms of material ambition. To the true server, all such opposition and resistance will but serve as added stimuli, rousing him to even greater exertion, inevitably leading him to new revelations of the joys of increasing inner vision and an ever expanding consciousness!

X

SACRIFICE

With the present dawning of the New Age the Hierarchy needs ever more intermediaries who are willing to sacrifice every form of self-interest, thus enabling them to serve as instruments for the guidance of humanity along new lines of thought and fresh patterns of activity.

Joyful Acquiescence

As with most concepts, several shades of meaning may be attached to the term sacrifice. To many it is the surrendering under some form of duress and therefore with varying degrees of regret, of something that would much rather be retained. In contrast to this approach, there is a far more exalted form of sacrifice which is not induced by constraint of any manner, but by an inner urge for expressing love, for freely giving and joyously sharing, without regarding the cost, of all that is at one's disposal in service of one's fellow men. Thus each can contribute his part, even though it may appear relatively insignificant, towards the realisation of the Divine Plan. Sacrifice is therefore the impulse to give, the act of completely surrendering the personality to the demands of the soul. This acquiescence should be accorded with the joy, serenity and knowledge that all that is conferred of one's time, possessions or energy, will be towards the fulfilment of his part of Destiny. It is only be relinquishing all in service of the Great Ones that perfect liberation can be achieved, thereby transmuting and raising the body of selfish desire to the intuitional or soul level, and thus attaining freedom from such emotional tribulations as anxiety and fear. The Goal is therefore reached by the path of renunciation or sacrifice, even though it might entail the renunciation of the so-called pleasures of life and all that is dear to the personality. It might also lead to the renunciation of fleeting earthly relationships and friendships, but it will most certainly provide the inner joys of revelation and recognition, also contributing towards the closer knitting of the bonds between kindred spirits and towards an ever expanding consciousness of being bathed in Supernal Light.

Surrender to the Absolute!

Therefore, sacrifice is actually the surrendering of the thwarted desires or self-will of the lower nature in conforming to the Divine Will as expressed through the soul. It is not necessarily the surrendering of all good things which in the past made life worth living, but the achieving of a higher objective without considering the relative loss to the material life. Thereby, a deeper understanding and recognition is gained of the energy of the will-to-good, an aspect of the underlying power of Love irresistibly guiding man along the Path of Return.

The concept of sacrifice therefore provides the student of Ancient Wisdom with another paradox, depending on the point of view that is entertained. Those acts of renunciation by the dedicated aspirant which may outwardly be regarded as a great and noble sacrifice, will actually represent no sacrifice to him, since such relinquishment or self-denial has become for him a spontaneous inner impulse from the soul, free from any form of compulsion or regret, bringing only happiness and joy in its consummation. So in the ordinary sense of the word, the true server makes no 'sacrifice', as that which is rendered or surrendered is offered freely and joyfully from a loving heart.

Every soul that is even faintly aware of the outlines of the Plan will be imbued with the spirit of sacrifice, sprouting from the very depths of being and blossoming as a yearning to give all, whether material or spiritual.

No service can ever prove truly effective unless performed with a sacrificial spirit, involving the renunciation of every aspect of the self, including personal desires, time and interests and the offering of these with an all-inclusive and unbiased love. Where the individual is acutely aware of his deed of sacrifice, either resenting the fact of somehow having been forced to perform it or else feeling smug and self-satisfied with his own magnanimity, the accomplished action may have positive results with regard to the recipients, but as far as the performer himself is concerned, it will prove of very little spiritual benefit and may even be harmful. No, true sacrifice can only be soul-inspired and therefore self-initiated, bestowed selflessly with love and compassion.

A Keynote of Human Existence

Although not commonly recognised today, sacrifice is one of the keynotes of human existence. It is frequently demonstrated by a spontaneous urge for relinquishing selfish personal interests to promote the well being of the group, community or whole. This note of Divine Love which is finding expression throughout the world with growing insistence, is concisely reflected in the motto 'Live TO let Live', which represents a vastly different approach to life than that which is reflected in the usual version which says 'Live AND let Live'.

The spirit of sacrifice is actually a manifestation of the loving Will of God, that divine energy which today is specifically being beamed towards humanity to assist in preparing man for the New Age which is now at hand. Those properly attuned and responsive to this supernal energy will exhibit its effects by an irresistible desire to participate in some way or degree in the Divine Sacrifice. This exalted Sacrifice is evinced not as a willingness to die but as a sublime desire to live for a sacred or ideal cause. This will to right living is the setting of an example to others by actively expressing the presence of the Inner Christ in daily living by sacrificing all personal interests for the welfare of others. Although the masses are not yet consciously aware of these spiritual energies, they are nonetheless distinctly responding to their influence. Unfortunately, this tendency is often exploited by politically inclined leaders, who by fine oratory or experienced emotional writing know how to appeal to and sway public opinion, calling for certain sacrifices to achieve their selfish political objectives. However, under right leadership and correct motivation, men can and will inevitably be led to tender the highest offerings to their ideals.

The principle of sacrifice is not limited to man alone. It similarly applies to more exalted Lives who on occasion may for instance sacrifice their ethereal existence by reverting to material levels of living in order to give of themselves and exert their influence towards the upliftment of lesser beings. This actually constitutes an essential aspect of the entire creative process, particularly that of the evolutionary progress which is stimulated by the sublime sacrifice and sharing of supernal knowledge and energies with the more humble. Thus man's evolution is largely grounded on the support and inspiration provided by the Hierarchy of Masters. Because humanity constitutes the link between the higher and the lower kingdoms of nature, one of the man's important responsibilities is to offer in his turn the powers with which he has been endowed towards the upliftment of the lower kingdoms.

In this light, the advent of the Christ two thousand years ago as well as His contemplated imminent return, receives new significance. No human being can possibly conceive of the nature and extent of the sacrifice involved in such a descent from spiritual levels to that of matter. Neither can the profundity of the love be fathomed with which the Christ must be imbued to allow him to proceed with His supreme act of renunciation.

For ages man has unconsciously been subject to the Law of Sacrifice and the underlying principles are generally accepted fairly readily. Regrettably, such acceptance does not necessarily imply its spontaneous application. Truly all world religions are founded on principles advocated by cosmic or etheric Beings who renounced their spiritual liberty by descending into the thraldom of matter, assuming human form in order to promulgate their specific message or teachings, thereby fulfilling their ordained mission as world Saviours. Thus the Christ, during his brief presence on Earth two thousand years ago, not only spread his message with regard to the all-encompassing power of love, but by the symbolic sacrifice of his physical life effectively made a further contribution towards the salvation, redemption and eventual liberation of humanity.

Often the individual is inclined to make a travesty of sacrifices by attempting to wield this law with the selfish intent of gaining some degree of personal salvation. Such abuse cannot, however, detract from or impair the basic principles which are of such vast and even universal import.

Universal Law

In the broadest aspect, the Law of Sacrifice actually governs both the creation and subsequent dissolution of universes and solar systems. In a narrower application, it determines the arrival and departure of races and nations with their leaders and rulers, the advent of the world Saviours and ensuing religions and, inevitably, the incarnation and re-incarnation of individual human beings. Sacrifice may therefore be regarded as a Divine Energy directed and controlled by the Divine Will and Purpose, resulting in some specific creative activity with corresponding effects. Our planet Earth is thus but the sacrificial manifestation of Deity, who for some Divine Purpose has temporarily invested the constituting matter with his life essence, thereby setting in motion the cyclic evolutionary system in which man is destined to play a leading role. In this evolutionary process man has been granted the opportunity of fulfilling a part and thereby hastening his own progress by voluntarily participating in the process of sacrifice, offering the powers at his disposal on the altar of human need, as well as to the needs of the evolving lives of the lower kingdoms of nature.

The final Purpose of Divine Sacrifice can never be fathomed by the limited comprehension of man. Apparently, the principal objectives tend towards the progressive development of consciousness, the simultaneous refining of form and the overall intensification of the life of every aspect of creation. As far as man is concerned, this originally was brought into expression by the "sacrifices of the Solar Angels', which led to 'individualisation' by lifting animal-man from the ranks of the animal to those of the human kingdom. This provided each individual with an immortal and reincarnating soul, with self-consciousness, a reasoning mind and understanding. By these gifts, man in turn became involved in his own sacrificial activities, finding expression in service to Spiritual Beings, by self-sacrificing help to fellow human beings and, finally, also in service to the lower forms of life.

Death is a form of sacrifice which is little understood by the average man, who still identifies himself with the life of the form without being conscious of the imprisoned soul. From the moment the position is reversed and he recognises and identifies with the soul instead of with the instrument through which it is functioning, there is a correspondingly improve understanding of the Law of Sacrifice, which in fact governs existence. This will lead to further recognition that the soul will, at the right time, deliberately decide to sacrifice its physical form, thus choosing the form to 'die' in order to liberate itself temporarily from its material shackles.

This trend towards sacrifice and the interchanging of material elements and energies between the various Kingdoms, is a spontaneous and normal occurrence throughout nature. The form structure of all material Kingdoms is primarily dependent on the minerals, while on a higher level, both the animal and human kingdoms rely largely on the sacrificed life and form of the vegetable world. Thus life is dependent on life, the lesser form being sacrificed to support the more advanced. The greater will however, in its turn, eventually make a reciprocal renunciation to provide the lesser with increased intelligence or consciousness, thereby contributing towards the evolution and raising of the lower forms of life.

Instinctive Urge

In man there exists an instinctive urge to salvage and sacrifice in order to redeem. This urge will vary widely in range and expression among individuals, depending on the stage of spiritual development, the influence of the specific Rays of Energy to which the various bodies are subjected, and the ruling environmental circumstances. Consequently this impulse will be displayed in many different ways. The urge to sacrifice is a spontaneous striving which is performed not for personal gain, but for altruistic purposes to provide the needed milk of human kindness. These underlying sacrificial instincts have always been present and have constituted the basis for man's spiritual evolution. However, with the present inflow of hierarchical forces, they are being accentuated and brought more forcibly to expression, though often remaining largely obscured by the forces of selfish desire which dominated mankind in the past. There is, however, definitely a growing tendency for man to turn his back upon "the world, the flesh and the devil", as expressed in the New Testament. In the past the higher values have been consciously sacrificed for the lower, but with the gradual awakening to reality and the entering onto the Path of Return, there is a conscious tendency developing to sacrifice the material values for the promotion of the spiritual. This urge to renounce the sordid for the exalted may often still indicate an insipient influence of an aspect of desire, but this no longer denotes the desire of the flesh, but rather the stirring of that which is Divine, the succession of the Inner Christ.

This instinctive inclination to sacrifice towards improvement of some nature, passes through an evolutionary process which, for the sake of clarity, might be divided into three comprehensive stages:

1) The stage where selfishness is predominant, where the forward striving is still of a grasping nature and governed by desire for that which is sensuous and material.
2) The stage where the spontaneous, altruistic nature is coming to expression. During the early phases, the tendency to sacrifice for alleviating the burdens of others might be somewhat selfishly motivated in an attempt to avoid the personal distress of having to observe the pain and suffering of others. However, this transitionary condition will inevitably be succeeded by genuine, disinterested, unselfish and soul-inspired service.
3) The culminating stage is reached with the complete and unconditional surrender and sacrifice of the lower self, thus "standing in spiritual being". This state will not be achieved until after the Third Initiation.

Realisation and Redemption

Those who wish to dedicate their lives to the redemption of mankind must therefore exhibit a spirit of utter self-sacrifice, a willingness for expending all they have to give of love and understanding, of time, energy and possessions and, yes, even of life, to achieve their ideals of service. This means the offering of everything at one's disposal to the

Lord of Life for the promotion of the One Work, with no thought of personal gain. Our Elder Brothers who are waiting to guide the inspired efforts of their younger brothers, still handicapped by the restraints of the flesh, are only too well aware of the many restrictions with which man on Earth has to cope. From their side, there is every compassion and understanding of man's problems, limitations, and even failures. Therefore, they do not expect perfection but are only looking for correctly motivated efforts, for the will to give and sacrifice, the will to love and understand and the will to serve! Where such spirit is evidenced, the Masters will keenly avail themselves of the offered instruments and the opportunity to serve will inevitably be provided. Therefore, rally and replenish your forces and, while forgetting about your personal interests, focus your vision anew on your future goal! Avoid idle gossip and criticism, envy and ambition! Instead, concentrate all your efforts on work, study, meditation and service, by love and renunciation!

During the present agonizing state of the world, humanity is in desperate need of the sacrificial offering of each individual aspirant. To each and everyone the opportunity is granted to pledge and surrender his all in the spirit of love, and with the knowledge that he is contributing his small share towards the realisation of the One Work and the redemption of Humanity!

APPENDIX

BOOKS BY THE TIBETAN
(DJWHAL KHUL)
through ALICE A. BAILEY

Book Ref. No.	Title	First Edition	Reference Edition	Pages
1.	*Initiation, Human and Solar*	1922	8th 1967	225
2.	*Letters on Occult Meditation*	1922	8th 1966	360
3.	*A Treatise on Cosmic Fire*	1925	6th 1964	1,283
4.	*A Treatise on White Magic*	1934	8th 1967	640
5.	*Discipleship in the New Age – Vol. I*	1944	6th 1966	790
6.	*Discipleship in the New Age – Vol. II*	1955	2nd 1955	768
7.	*The Problems of Humanity*	1947	3rd 1964	181
8.	*The Reappearance of The Christ*	1948	3rd 1960	189
9.	*The Destiny of Nations*	1949	2nd 1960	152
10.	*Glamour: A World Problem*	1950	3rd 1967	272
11.	*Telepathy and the Etheric Vehicle*	1950	3rd 1963	197
12.	*Education in the New Age*	1954	1st 1954	153
13.	*The Externalisation of the Hierarchy*	1957	2nd 1958	701
	A Treatise on the Seven Rays			
14.	*Vol. I- Esoteric Psychology I*	1936	5th 1967	430
15.	*Vol. II- Esoteric Psychology II*	1942	2nd 1960	751
16.	*Vol. III- Esoteric Astrology*	1951	5th 1965	695
17.	*Vol. IV- Esoteric Healing*	1953	4th 1967	715
18.	*Vol. V- The Rays and the Initiations*	1960	2nd 1965	769

NOTE

Reference Example: A reference number, such as for instance (12-135/6) at the end of a quotation, would refer to a quotation taken from "*Education in the New Age*" (12) starting on page 135, and continued on page 136.

164

Bibliography Aart Jurriaanse

1. Own works

a) Afrikaans

- **Uit Oupa se Dagboek** [From Grandfather's Diary]
  Somerset-West, without year (1970s), Sun Center, Sentrum vir
  Esoteriese Filosofie [Center for Esoteric Philosophy]

- **Waarvandaan en Waarheen? : 'n Inleiding tot die wyshede van
  ouds geklee in modern drag: vir die soekende jong oues en ou
  jonges** [Whence and Whither? : An Introduction into the
  Ancient Wisdom Teachings, clothed in modern language for the
  seeking young at heart and the young. (South African Service
  Unit)]
  Johannesburg 1973 (Suid-Afrikaanse Diens-Eeenheid)

b) English

- **Of Life and Other Worlds**
  - Pretoria 1974 (Private Publication); Craighall 1974 and 1993,
    South Africa, World Unity & Service, South Africa
  - Frankfurt am Main 2026, ISBN 978-3-949550-32-4
    Verlag Hans-Jürgen Maurer (Bridges Publishing)

- **Bridges**
  Pretoria 1978, Published by BRIDGES TRUST:
  - Somerset West 1980, 1981, 1985, 1989, 1994, by Sun Centre,
    Pretoria 1986
  - Freiburg im Breisgau 2001 (revised edition, Hardcover)
    ISBN 978-3-929345-11-7
    Verlag Hans-Jürgen Maurer (Bridges Publishing)
  - Frankfurt am Main 2026 (revised edition, Paperback),
    ISBN 978-3-929345-98-8,
    Verlag Hans-Jürgen Maurer (Bridges Publishing)

- **All is Relative: A Revelation of Man's Cosmic Connections**
  - Somerset West (without year,1980s), Inner Space Publishers;
  - Freiburg im Breisgau 2004, ISBN 978-3-929345-21-6
    Verlag Hans-Jürgen Maurer (Bridges Publishing)

- **Life – Now and Hereafter**
  - South Africa 1987 (private publication);
  - Freiburg im Breisgau 2007 (without „Part II – Exctracts [from
    other authors' books]). ISBN 978-929345-25-4 – out of print.
  - Frankfurt am Main 2026 (Complete) ISBN 978-3-929345-60-5
    Verlag Hans-Jürgen Maurer (Bridges Publishing)

c) Translations into other languages

BRIDGES:

German
- **Philosophie der Synthese: Eine Einführung in die zeitlosen
  Weisheitslehren**
  - München 2002, neue aspekte Verlag, ISBN 3-9806579-3-0 – out
    of print
  - Frankfurt am Main 2014, ISBN 978-3-929345-28-5,
    Verlag Hans-Jürgen Maurer

Italian
- **Ponti** (2 Bände) Vol. 1, Spigno Saturnia 2003;
  Vol. 2, Spigno Saturnia 2004; Edizioni Crisalide
  ISBN Vol. 1 978-887183-130-5, Vol. 2 978-887183-156-5

2. Compilations from the Works of Alice A. Bailey

a) English

- **Ponder on This**
  London 1971, Lucis Trust (numerous printings, several languages)
- **Serving Humanity**
  London 1972, Lucis Trust (numerous printings, several languages)

- **Prophecies** [D. K.]
  - Craighall 1977, South Africa, Wold Unity & Service;
  - Edited for the 21st century by Johann Grobler: Johannesburg 2008
  - 2nd printing 2009, Publishing House: Lead the Field,
    ISBN 978-0-620-41982-6
  - 3rd edition 2012 by Johann Grobler: The Tibetan Master,
    PROPHECIES, The Tibetan Master, Create Space, Charleston SC,
    USA, ISBN 978-0-620-52452-0

- **The Soul, the Quality of Life**
  London 1974, Lucis Trust (numerous printings)

- **Reference guide to the teachings of D.K. by Alice A. Bailey**
  Craighall 1978, South Africa, World Unity & Service

b) French

- **Les Sept Rayons d'Énergie** [The Seven Rays of Energy], Montre-
  al (without year).
  Available online as a free of charge PDF: www.taraquebec.org

3. Unpublished own works

- **The Lighted Way**

4. Unpublished Compilations from the Works of Alice A. Bailey

- **Thought**

- **The Seven Rays of Energy** (Unpublished in English. The French edition is available online. See 2.b.)

- **Silent Guides**